SCHOOL
OF MAN

ISBN: 978-19-5-315349-4

Published by

LIFESTYLE
ENTREPRENEURS
P R E S S

If you are interested in publishing through Lifestyle Entrepreneurs Press, write to: *Publishing@LifestyleEntrepreneursPress.com*

Publications or foreign rights acquisition of our catalog books.
Learn More: *www.LifestyleEntrepreneursPress.com*

Printed in the USA

SCHOOL OF MAN

A MAN'S GUIDE TO LIVING, LOVING & LEGACY

COLE RODGERS
with **GUY CHOATE**

When the image of a man-eating beast travels through the optic nerve and into the visual cortex, the brain relays an urgent message to the body: *run!* That's what normal people do, but normal is over-rated. Lion chasers don't run away; lion chasers run to the roar. They don't see a five-hundred-pound problem; they seize opportunity by the mane. They don't take flight; they fight to the death for their dreams.

-Mark Batterson
Chase the Lion

CONTENTS

INTRODUCTION

My name is Cole Rodgers. You aren't supposed to know me. I'm just a regular man, and I don't have everything figured out, but I haven't stopped trying. That continued pursuit is what I suggest you take from this book if you're going to take anything. The rest of it is mine and I wouldn't suggest you try to lay claim to any of it.

There's a lot of good, but there's also a lot of bad. And I've earned it all.

I'm going to tell you about my experience in the hopes that you'll be able to get a better grasp of your own, but make no mistake, this book is not meant to be a quick-fix for all of your problems. Or any of them. It's the opposite. This book is here to tell you that the fix is hard, that it's going to take significant effort, and that the perception you've carried with you your entire life about what it means to be a man is probably wrong.

Masculinity, femininity, and everything in between has become much more complex in recent years—or at least society has learned to talk about it in a much more complex way—but I'm not attempting to join that conversation. Frankly, I'm not

1

equipped to. And even more frankly, I don't care to. I'm fine with anyone who wants to read my book to gain perspective—men, women, and whatever else is out there—but I'm here to talk about what I understand. I'm here to talk to the men who—like me—were taught to emulate the qualities they saw in men like John Wayne, James Bond, and Clint Eastwood. Men who were clearly dominant, successful, and good looking. Men who were simple, yet held a surprisingly unachievable standard.

It never occurred to me that one of those role models is a fictional character, and the other two might as well be. No matter how hard I tried, I was never going to be on a level with those men, so I was left feeling inferior to the man I wanted to be. We all were. I spent a good portion of my adult life coming to terms with that, and it was hard, but I've come out on the other side alive and feeling better about my place in this world than I ever have. That's about all I could ever ask for.

I am Cole Rodgers. You aren't supposed to know me. I'm just a regular man with a better understanding than I used to have about what it means to live, to love, and to build a legacy for my family that I can be proud of. Everything I write in the pages that follow is an admittance—a reminder to myself—that to be a man means you must have the courage to break yourself down to be able to build yourself up. How and when and why you finally decide to break yourself down is different for every one of us, but the fundamental principles remain the same.

Embrace your vulnerabilities. Embrace your truths. Chase the lion.

PART ONE

A HISTORY

1

SOMETHING'S MISSING

When Adam McPike's ex-wife picked up and moved from Little Rock, Arkansas to the northwest corner of the state, she took their two children with her. She took him to court in an attempt to gain full custody of the kids. Even though they'd been divorced for two years, he felt the pain of divorce all over again when the legal system put his character back on trial, even though the only new relevant life event that had transpired was his ex's desires to uproot their family without telling him. She tried to make the case that since he didn't even live in the same part of the state with them, he didn't need custody. So he got a place near the kids and began spending half his time living in a house in Northwest Arkansas, and half in Little Rock in the center of the state. He kept a corporate apartment in Little Rock's River Market District downtown.

He proved to the court that he's a worthy father and was granted joint legal custody, but suffice it to say the whole debacle turned his life upside-down. A divorce already makes life hard, but things got progressively more complicated for Adam.

He's a salesman for a masonry materials supply company, so he travels a large portion of the state selling stone and brick to commercial organizations. Adam's likable and easy to talk to, which is probably why he ended up in sales, but the demands of balancing his job responsibilities with the circumstances of his personal life began to take a toll on him. To the point that a couple of years ago, Adam woke up in his apartment in Little Rock contemplating suicide.

He pulled himself together and got out of bed. He threw on some shorts and a tee-shirt, and some running shoes. He had a regular jogging route that he thought could do him some good. He ran down past the Clinton Presidential Library, across the Arkansas River via a pedestrian bridge, along the river trail, and back over to the Joe T. Robinson Auditorium, which serves the city as a venue for national performing arts acts. He usually continues down President Clinton Avenue back toward his apartment, but for whatever reason that morning, he made an early right turn, and that's where he saw two grown men up the street, carrying what looked like a log—a tree trunk, stripped of its limbs. They could've been timber men or construction workers if they'd worn work boots, safety vests, and hard hats, but instead, they wore workout clothes like him. And even if they'd been dressed like lumberjacks, it wouldn't have made sense for them to be in downtown Little Rock.

His curiosity was piqued, but he didn't feel comfortable talking to them—strange, given that he's generally comfortable talking to anyone—so he ran the block again, trying to work up his courage.

By the time he came around again, the two men had set the log down to take a break, and Adam had found the courage he needed to initiate a conversation with strangers.

"What are y'all doing?" Adam asked.

The men looked up at him. One had gray hair and a baby face, the other wore a short, groomed beard with gray hair on his chin. They were fit, but not obnoxiously so. The man with the beard stared back at Adam with an intimidating look as if to say, "What in the hell do you think we're doing?"

"How's it going?" the other man piped up with a big smile. "We're carrying this log. Taking it down there to the gym."

Adam studied them some more. He was born and raised in Arkansas and maintained general Southern hospitality at all times, so he said, "Do y'all want some help?"

The two men looked at each other, then back at Adam.

"If you want to get on here," they said, "You're free to."

So Adam put a shoulder under the log with the two men and the three of them continued on down the street together toward the Above & Beyond CrossFit gym. On the way, the baby-faced man introduced himself as Ed Green. The bearded man was Jeff Powell. Adam enjoyed the conversation, and surprisingly, he enjoyed the shared task of carrying the weighty log through downtown Little Rock with men he didn't know. The two men had carried the log from the Arkansas State Capitol building—a two-mile haul altogether—with a half-mile remaining when Adam threw his own shoulder under the hefty burden with them.

When they got to the gym, Jeff pulled Adam aside and told him carrying the log wasn't just about an ordinary CrossFit exercise. It was part of something else, something bigger, something called the School of Man. Jeff described a physical and

7

mental program that intimidated Adam, but it also thrilled and intrigued him. Afterward, Jeff offered to give Adam a ride back to his apartment, but Adam declined. He needed to walk alone with his thoughts to process what had just happened. But regardless of everything else he thought about the experience, he could tell *something* had just happened.

He liked that two men who didn't know him from any other Adam—I guess you could say—were willing to invite him in to share their goal. They were willing to take a chance on trusting him to carry his share of the enormous weight they shouldered together. Adam needed people in his life who weren't afraid of hard tasks and could trust him to help them with those tasks. He needed people like Jeff and Ed. Ironically, by volunteering to carry weight with those two strangers, Adam freed himself of the metaphorical weight he'd woken up carrying that morning that was so heavy it almost drove him to want to kill himself.

He needed some guys who would be there for him and hold him accountable, without judgment—not just when everything in life was going well, but also during the low points of his life. There were plenty of people around during the periods of his life when he was winning, at the top, but once you go through things like divorces and have to face similar adversities, you lose people. Adam lost a lot of friends because they were forced to choose sides—and that's not to place blame—it's just the nature of such things. (More than 40 percent of School of Man participants have gone through a divorce, and a large portion of those guys have never met their dad. I don't think that's a coincidence.) Unfortunately, it left him more alone than he'd ever been. Especially because he couldn't devote all of himself to a single community due to the fact that he was traveling back and forth to different parts of the state all the time. He had plenty of people he could call in a pinch and check in, but when it came to people who were a steady presence in his life, that he could see face-to-face on a regular basis, Adam was isolated.

He saw something he lacked in the faces and body language of Jeff and Ed carrying the log that morning, and if he didn't absolutely need that, he at least knew he wanted it. He spent the walk to his apartment contemplating whether or not he could participate in School of Man, wondering if he was good enough to see it through. By the time he reached his apartment, he knew he owed it to his future to try. So he went to schoolofman.live, he took a look at our Facebook page, then he sent me an email. I called him and we talked for a good half-hour about what he was after and what we could provide.

Adam filled out the application and we accepted him into School of Man Class 003.

I've already told you where he was when he started the program, but after nearly a year of our curriculum, which involves physical training, mental training and meditation, and a lot of relationship development with a lot of other men, he finished the program with a new kind of inner strength and confidence that he now carries with him everywhere he goes. He always had a purpose, but now he knows he can face that purpose with his head held high. He accepts that life isn't always going to be easy, but he also understands he has the ability to endure it until the hard part's over.

"It's just like the crucible," Adam said, referring to the hellish 56-hour event every School of Man class must endure to earn their Phoenix. But more on that later. Before I get too far into what any of that is, let me tell you about how it was born, and to understand that you'll need to know a little about me.

Just like Adam, I lacked something I needed.

2

HOME

I grew up in central Arkansas in a small city called Conway, but in the summers and on a lot of weekends, my parents would gather me and my sister up and drive the 30 miles north to Catholic Point, which is a community so small it doesn't even have its own Wikipedia page in this era when everything has its own Wikipedia page. That community's there, though, I promise, and it's mostly populated by people I'm related to.

My mom grew up there with her six brothers and sisters. There are no subdivisions, no gated communities. Mostly it's just a row of residences about a quarter-mile long that begins with my grandmother's house and ends with my uncle's. My uncles and my grandfather built those houses with their own hands, and in between each of them are small fields or a shared garden we've all spent time working at one point or another.

My Uncle Sonny raised beagles he used for rabbit hunting and he kept them in a dog pen behind my grandmother's house, next to the chicken coop, which was home to about a dozen hens and a rooster at any given time. There was a barn full of hay, stored potatoes, and some farming equipment—a tractor and such. We had what we called a horse stable, and it served that purpose, but it wasn't but a piece of barbed wire strung from one post to another. Back behind all that sat a small pond and a hundred wooded acres that belonged to us.

My family beat a footpath between the houses. My cousins and I referred to it as *the path*, and we used it as much as anybody when we ran back and forth from my grandmother's house to my aunt's, then to my uncle's—headed to the garden or in search of Muscadine vines or to try and shoot the basketball through the hoop that hung on the light pole. We were fond of taking an old shop rag and wrapping it in duct tape as tightly as we could until it could function as a decent substitute for a baseball. We had our own makeshift baseball diamond out beside my aunt's house. With oak trees and the swing set and clothes lines serving as bases or foul lines and a tree root marking the pitcher's mound, it wasn't exactly ready for regulation play, but it served our purposes pretty well.

My grandmother hung her laundry out to dry, a dog barked in the distance, a chicken clucked around the corner, and the wind always blew just right through the trees. In my grandmother's house, on any given day, I'd be hit with the aroma of something that would make my mouth water—fresh pasta, fried chicken, or gravy, maybe. I was taught early on when I entered the house that I should kiss my grandmother, kiss my aunts, then immediately walk to the living room to look every man in the eye and shake his hand. I found the act to be intimidating for a long time, but I learned to see the importance of it as

I got older, and I still believe in looking a man in the eye when I shake his hand.

My family is Catholic, so the walls in Grandma's house also displayed prominently the images of the saints and the Virgin Mary and Jesus Christ. And if it's not obvious by now, family was a big deal to us, so Grandma also proudly displayed a picture of our family tree—all of our names written over the images of bright red apples. Each of us was a fruit from the life labors of my grandmother and grandfather. My family gave me everything I needed in life to be successful, they gave me an idyllic upbringing, and above all else, they taught me how to do the right thing. If my moral compass ever strayed—and it did—it was never through the fault of my upbringing.

I had plenty of male role models. For a time, there were the "big boys," which was my older cousins, and then there were the "little boys," which was the category that I fell into. As a little boy, I watched in awe as the big boys played games with a passion and fire that was infectious. The big boys never took it easy on us—on the baseball diamond or elsewhere. We argued and fought as equals, though the big boys were much bigger than the little boys and could physically dominate us whenever they wanted to. They taught me a lot of lessons, but the most valuable was that I had to do the work if I wanted to be a part of the team. Even if it wasn't always fun. If I wanted a turn at bat, I had to do my time fielding balls. And once I put in the work, just like the big boys, I could celebrate my home runs and everyone would celebrate with me. There's a camaraderie that existed there that I've probably been pursuing ever since.

Every Fourth of July we still have a tape ball game, even though we're grown men now. We've expanded the field and there are more players than there used to be, but it's the same game. We still talk the same trash, and we still laugh our asses off when someone does something out of character, or in character, for that matter. After the game, we turn it over to the kids and they play. It's a family tradition that I hope will last as long as my family does, and I also hope it will keep teaching valuable lessons from one generation to next.

None of us are so smart that we can't still learn a lesson or two. Let me tell you about one of my greatest lessons that I didn't learn until it was almost too late, but like a lot of things in life, someone was there to teach it to me right in the nick of time.

3

UNFUCK YOURSELF

Winter was closing in on us in Arkansas—the sky was graying, the breeze had a cold nip to it. It was the kind of weather that pulls men by the handfuls to the deer woods and television sets to watch college football. But on the day I'm talking about now, I was neither hunting, nor rooting for my Arkansas Razorbacks. That day, I sat looking into the eyes of a 16-year veteran of the United States Marine Corps named JC McDaniel.

"Cole, you need to unfuck yourself," he said.

I hadn't joined the Corps, and I wasn't in any sort of military training, but I was beginning to learn some hard truths about myself.

Ashley and I had been married for almost four years at that time. We had two children—Ava Madison and Landon—and a lot of problems, most of which I had caused. Me and my ego.

My family has a really low divorce rate, and I had no intention of tarnishing that record, but even if I could somehow come to terms myself with wanting a divorce—which I couldn't (and won't)—one of the things I love about my wife is that she's a grinder. She has no quit in her. She wouldn't let me divorce her.

Before meeting Ashley, I'd only been in two serious relationships in my life up to that point—a high school girlfriend who broke my heart, and a college girlfriend who also broke my heart. After that second heartbreak, I decided to reroute the energy I'd been putting into relationships to concentrate more on my professional successes. I found making money to be way more rewarding than cultivating a pattern of heartbreak.

Making money became everything to me. It was a way for me to measure success using quantifiable goals. My dad did me a solid and got me a job interview as a benefits counselor for a large insurance company. The job would require me to spend more than 200 days a year on the road educating teachers and municipal workers about the benefits they had available to them. It would also require me to move to Nashville, Tennessee, a good five hours from home. My tightly knit family generally liked to stay together in central Arkansas, but the opportunity to go forth and do great things excited me, so when they offered me the position, I packed up the few things I had and moved to the Music City.

I was 21 years old, in a new place, with a new job. I moved in with a guy named Jake Molder, who was living in Nashville at the time. I'd gone to high school and college with Jake's younger brother, and he helped me get acclimated to the city a little, but ultimately, I didn't know anyone there. I wanted to fit in, and I felt like an underdog trying to make it in a world I didn't have a real perspective on yet, so I tried my best to emulate what everyone around me was doing. They were making money, and they were spending it. They partied all night long and then were eager to wake up the next morning and keep rocking and rolling so we could still be the best at what we did. We had the mentality on fine display in the movie The Wolf of Wall Street. Conversations started and ended with "How much money are you making?" To keep up with everyone else, I felt like I had to embrace that mentality, too. So I did. But that kind of lifestyle isn't sustainable and I knew that, even as I was determined to keep up with everyone else, so I began looking for ways to make it easier.

Before that, when I was at a house party in college, someone said, "Hey, take this," and handed me a little pill. I had always been anti-drugs. Marijuana didn't do much for me in the few times I tried it, and the idea of anything else sounded pretty stupid, so I relied on alcohol when I wanted to check out of reality. But when someone handed me that pill I didn't think twice about popping it into my mouth and swallowing it. I don't remember who gave it to me. I honestly don't even remember if it actually was a house party. I could've been in the library studying for a test. It all runs together in my memory now, but at some point during those years, I tried Adderall that had not been prescribed to me.

Adderall is how the pharmaceutical industry answered the call to deal with attention deficit hyperactivity disorder—something doctors basically decided to diagnose my entire generation with. Put simply, the pill is an amphetamine that acts as a stimulant to settle the hyperactive mind so the patient can focus on the task at hand. I never got diagnosed with ADHD, but I discovered very quickly that Adderall could save my ass when I got lazy and didn't feel like studying for a test until the last minute. I didn't need a prescription for it because everyone had it. And it felt innocent enough at the time because most of the time when I took it, I got the things done that I needed to get done for school. I passed the test or wrote the paper. Academic accomplishments didn't feel like it could ever be categorized as drug abuse.

I am already a naturally charged individual. I'm goal-oriented and always looking to take things to the next level. I didn't understand my friends and classmates who got into muscle relaxers and smoking pot because I didn't want to feel subdued; I wanted to go faster, to get more things done, to achieve at the highest levels. And that's what I thought I was doing when I got to Nashville.

As I said, I felt like the underdog, and there's more than one reason for that, but one of the reasons had to do with coming from having been raised in a small town and then trying to make it in a big city. A lot of my friends stayed in our hometown—some were accomplishing things, some weren't—but I couldn't get it out of my head that I wanted to return home one day and show them all what I had accomplished.

I wanted to show everyone that I had gone out into the world and made it on my own. I wanted to pick up everyone's bar tabs and thus prove to people how great I was at doing life. And if I'm being honest with myself, it wasn't just that I wanted to show my friends what I had accomplished—I also wanted to show my family. Especially my father.

I'm a mama's boy and always have been, but there's something about men that keeps us in perpetual pursuit of our dads' validation. A man will always be in search of that moment—no matter what age he is—when his father will look him in the eye and say, "I'm proud of you, son."

Ashley and I recently made the difficult decision to hold our son Landon back a year in school. Coming to terms with having to repeat kindergarten when of all his friends are moving on to first grade has been hard on him. It's been hard on all of us, but especially Landon and Ashley, who did everything she could to help him excel more. Among other things, we got him a tutor and a speech therapist, but Ashley still battled with the idea that she had somehow failed him as a mother.

I know Ashley's a good mother—among other reasons—because Ava Madison who is 12 months older than Landon immediately volunteered to repeat her grade too, so she and Landon wouldn't be split up more than the year that they already are. There's some leadership qualities on display there that we teach in the School of Man, but we'll get to that later.

Right now I want to talk about Landon and how even though he's going through a lot of emotional soul searching as a kindergartener—way before he is probably emotionally equipped to—he came to me and said he wanted to have a boys' night. I was lying in bed in nothing but my compression shorts, which is what I sleep in. Landon pulled off his shirt and shorts and we both lied there in our underwear and watched *Aquaman* because that's what he said he wanted to do. But at one point in the movie he turned and looked at me and we got to what he really wanted.

He said, "Dad, are you proud of me?"

Of course I melted and said, "Absolutely, I'm proud of you."

Landon's just a kindergartener, but even after men grow up, there is still a little boy inside of all of us who just wants to hear his father tell us that he is proud of us. Sometimes the pressure of that feeling drives us to do stupid things because we don't know how to handle it. We don't realize that pressure is a privilege. When we haven't reached a certain emotional maturity yet, the pursuit of trying to make our fathers proud of us can paradoxically drive us to do the very things that won't make our fathers proud of us at all.

That's the situation I found myself in when I lived in Nashville, crushing up Adderall to snort, which I thought I needed to be able to soar with the eagles at night and still produce the results at work during the day so as to continue my proverbial climb up the corporate ladder. For my job, I traveled to these remote towns to work with teachers in the schools there, communicating to them about the benefits they had available, but I also felt like I had this persona that I needed to uphold. I needed to be able to tell the friends I had made about the women I had found to sleep around with.

To admit that now hurts me because that's not me. That's not who my family raised me to be. That was just a mask I'd learned to wear. I knew it in the moment, just as well as I know it now that it's forever preserved in the distant past. I learned to wear lots of masks so that I could succeed in whatever game I was playing. The root of it all was always that I wanted to bring home a vault full of trophies—in whatever form they took—so I could show them to my dad and ask the exact same thing Landon asked me, "Dad, are you proud of me?"

The weird thing is, my dad never set that kind of standard for me. He never told me to go out and collect a bunch of trophies, but that didn't alleviate my desire to do that for him. So goes the nature of fathers and sons, I suppose. All he ever asked of me was to be a good human being and to make my best effort in everything I did. And that's all I will ever ask of Landon, and having to repeat kindergarten will have no bearing on his ability to make me proud. Now that I'm on the other side of a father-son relationship, I can see it more clearly. But at the time, I didn't understand what it means to love as a father.

My dad came from nothing. He grew up in Oklahoma and his dad worked in the oil fields in the 1950s. That was a seven-day-a-week job, no matter what the weather looked like. The oil rigs have no idea about Christmas or Thanksgiving or your kid's birthday or when someone is graduating from high school—the rig does not care. So Pawpaw was on a rig somewhere, all the time. Not one time did he ever see my dad play in a ball game or anything like that because he felt the necessity was to work to make money to pay the bills. The factor Pawpaw's philosophy didn't take into account was that when he got paid, there were a lot of honky tonks and beer joints and liquor stores between the oil fields and the house, so a lot of that money he got paid never made it home in time to pay the bills. Meanwhile, my grandmother was working two jobs—on the line at a frozen waffle plant at night and waiting tables for tips at a diner on the weekends—while trying to raise three kids. So Dad witnessed some genuine marital battles, for sure, when he was a kid.

My grandparents separated when my dad was nine years old and divorced the next year. His mother raised him as best she could as a single parent. Unfortunately, absentee fathers are as prevalent today as they probably always have been. Mothers are forced to step up to the challenge and children are forced to look elsewhere for positive male influencers.

His mother had to play the role of both Mom and Dad for him and my uncles without many resources. She went above and beyond the call of duty to make sure their family had a place to live and food to eat. They ate a lot of pinto beans, fried potatoes, a piece of cornbread, and a slice of onion because it was low-cost and it went a long way, but they were grateful to have it.

A few years later, my grandmother married a guy who was about to get out of the Air Force and they were going to move to Little Rock, but my dad was a senior in high school and the move would've meant he'd have to repeat a lot of his senior year. Instead, he moved in with Pawpaw and his wife in Enid, Oklahoma, so he could finish up by going to school three hours a day. But even though he lived with Pawpaw, it didn't mean my dad didn't hold a grudge against him for the way he had more or less abandoned their family and left the mother of his children to take on all the parenting responsibilities.

When all the other kids had dads at the ballgame or the school function, Dad didn't, and it stoked the anger inside him toward Pawpaw. It wasn't until the late 1970s, when Dad was putting in 70 hours a week and working nearly 200 days straight as a district manager for Frito Lay that tension really began to ease between him and Pawpaw. Possibly because Pawpaw recognized himself in my dad's work ethic. Granted, Dad wasn't blowing his family's rent money in honky tonks, but still, Pawpaw always respected people who had a strong work ethic, and when he respected Dad, it made reconciling the relationship easier. It also didn't hurt that his wife, my dad's stepmother, thought healing that relationship was the right thing to do. She dragged him toward rebuilding the relationship with his son and by the time my grandfather passed away, there was a decent relationship between them.

Despite his own relationship with his father, my dad was a good father to me and my sister, and he has always loved my mother, which is how they've stayed together for nearly 40 years. He taught me how to behave in a marriage and gave me a good example of how to take care of a family. We were middle class and I never really wanted for anything. Dad always supported me in everything he did. He showed up to all of my athletic events, he'd shoot baskets with me in the driveway, and he'd hit me ground balls so I could practice fielding them if I asked him to.

As I said, we're Catholic, and the Catholic church has a ban on contraceptives, so my cousins who were sexually active ended up having unwanted pregnancies. As a result, I tended to shy away from sex as a teenager because I knew I didn't want that. But when I eventually lost my virginity at age 18, the girl accused me of taking advantage of her. She threatened to call the police. I knew I hadn't taken advantage of her, but I had no proof and that scared the hell out of me. I tried talking to my friends about it, but they basically just said, "Fuck her, man, let's go get drunk," which was not a realistic way to approach the problem. I didn't know what to do, and I was depressed about it, so I talked to my dad.

We were sitting in my 1994 green Chevrolet short-bed pick-up truck and we'd just put the family Christmas tree into it. I told him the situation I had gotten myself into and tears came streaming out of my face. I'd only been that vulnerable with my father maybe once or twice before because being vulnerable like that when I was trying to be John Wayne? It felt like weakness, and I didn't know how my father would react to his son showing weakness. Of course, now I recognize what my father knew then—that tears do not equal weakness. And Dad did what dads should do.

He reached over and hugged me and told me he loved me.

In a way, I felt like that was the beginning of my adult relationship with my father. That's when I began to really feel connected to him—man to man. Showing vulnerability allowed that relationship to blossom, and looking back, that should've been an eye-opener.

There are a lot of men in this world who don't have the opportunity to build a relationship with their father. I got lucky and it's my relationship with my father that helped me embrace my own manhood, authentically. Or at least it did eventually. As men, it's vital that we have this kind of relationship with other men, be they our actual biological fathers or not.

4

REINVENTION

After almost five years in Nashville, I found myself to be a lonely shell of person. I knew I needed to get away from the lifestyle I'd created for myself if I was ever going to make the change I knew I needed in my life. Nothing could have put that into perspective more than the death of my grandmother and a subsequent storm that wiped out entire sections of the family property where I had played as a child.

I went home and assessed the property damage with my cousins. Parts of the property were unrecognizable to the versions I had grown accustomed to in my memory. We debated how the family would recover from the loss of Grandma, who had been such a pillar of strength and connectedness for us all. We didn't know what life after Grandma could possibly look like. I sat at my grandmother's kitchen table, where I had enjoyed so many family meals, and I searched online for a new place to live outside of Nashville, a new city to escape to.

I decided to move to Raleigh, North Carolina, a place in which I had never really spent much time outside of a trip or two for work, but I knew moving to Raleigh could be another stepping stone in my life and my career. Searching for a new apartment gave me a chance to take my mind off the uncertainty and grief I didn't know how to maturely deal with yet.

I fantasized about my future life in Raleigh, where I knew no one—I didn't even know where my office was. I could reinvent myself, keeping all of the parts of me that made me great at my job, but ditching all the unhealthy aspects of the life I'd created in Nashville. No more masks, no more partying all night, no more drugs, no more one-night stands that left me feeling empty. I could feel a war raging inside me between the life I had been living and the life I wanted to live. My past and my future. My fraudulent behavior and my authentic self. I couldn't wait to get back to the person my family had raised me to be.

My new landlord accepted the deposit for my apartment in North Raleigh over the phone while I sat there at my grandmother's table. I'd never even seen the apartment, but I didn't have to because I was purchasing more than the physical space; I bought myself a fresh start. Or so I hoped.

The corporate ladder was waiting for me in Raleigh and I set a goal to climb it as a way to eventually get back home to central Arkansas and be near my family, and maybe raise a family of my own should the opportunity present itself. I didn't know exactly how it would happen, but I had every confidence it would if I could keep my head down and work my ass off. No bullshit distractions.

So that's what I did, getting up, getting dressed, going to the office, putting in a full day, eating dinner, going to sleep.

I regularly put in more than sixty hours a week, week after week, and I enjoyed it. I was proving—to myself more than anyone else—that I could develop healthy relationships with hard-working people to accomplish big things at work, and that I deserved to live that kind of life.

Until I hit a wall.

I never saw it coming before I ran smack into it. And then I did what my natural instinct tells me to do, which is to sabotage myself into failure. I got complacent with my self-discipline right about the time I also experienced a case of the workaholic's burn-out—those two things often arrive together, hand-in-hand. I began spending my Friday nights at a bar not far from my apartment where I met people I had nothing in common with, but it initially alleviated some of the loneliness I harbored inside. Alcohol and loneliness are a dangerous combination, and before I knew it, I developed a weekend routine that found me binge-drinking my way through Friday nights and lazing about my apartment until Monday snuck up on me too quickly, but I had no choice but to show up for work, feeling physically groggy and mentally dull. Friday night after Friday night looked exactly the same. And Monday morning after Monday morning looked exactly the same.

I spent enough time at the bar that I got to know some of the staff. One night the bar owner invited me to come back to his house to play Wii Bowling with a group of people. I didn't really know anyone there, but I joined in and was thankful to hang out. When it was my turn to bowl, I did what I do and gave it everything I had, really putting some power into throwing the Wii remote. The problem was, I *actually threw* the remote and sent it flying through the $2,000 big screen television.

I ruined the party not fifteen minutes after I got there, had to replace the television the next day, and was still remarkably lonely. I was so lonely that I agreed to take a road trip with a guy I barely knew from the bar because I thought it might be a good time—that's how I sold it to myself—but put into the perspective of reality, I had let myself be conned into riding shotgun for a stranger who was in the middle of a drug deal. I had no business being there with that person, had nothing to gain, yet there I was.

I know now that this is exactly the kind of self-sabotaging loop I like to put myself into. I work hard to succeed in my career, then find a way to sabotage things—I dip back to a lower standard so that I can achieve beyond it again to relive that natural high I get from success. I yo-yo up and down, rather than continuing to climb even higher, and that hurts my ultimate potential. I know that now, but it cost me a lot before I learned to understand and recognize the patter. It almost cost me everything I love.

I'm lucky enough to have a family that reminds me to stay grounded and keep things in perspective. My parents and a set of aunts and uncles travelled to Appalachia where we spent a few days at a rented cabin in Asheville, North Carolina and another in Pigeon Forge, Tennessee. It was the fall, the air was crisp, and the tree leaves were displaying their full range of many colors.

I sat in that cabin in the mountains with my Uncle Buck, who was battling Stage IV brain cancer at the time and I was in awe of how happy he seemed. Despite his dire outlook, he remained positive and kept a smile on his face. He never complained about his unfair circumstances, but he also wasn't suppressing his emotions as he wasn't ashamed to cry in front of me.

That time with my family, that retreat from my sad and lonely life in Raleigh, made me appreciate the people I come from so much. We played golf in the mountains, toured the 8,000-acre Biltmore estate, and spent time roaming shops together. On the night before they drove back to Arkansas, the reality of my situation set in again. The thought of going back to what had become my daily grind crushed me. I hadn't cried like that since I was boy, but I wept like a child in front of my parents and my aunts and uncles because I didn't want them to leave. I'd missed their love and affection because I didn't have that on a regular basis anymore. No matter how many hours I worked, it didn't earn me the love and affection I needed, the love and affection I had been given by them since the day I was born, the love and affection we all need to be at our best.

My parents felt sympathy for me, but we all knew they couldn't stay. They had their own lives back in Arkansas and I was a grown-ass man that had to build a life on his own, too. My mom and dad had already given me all the tools I needed to do that, and we all knew it was up to me to use them. They couldn't make my loneliness disappear—I would have to find a way to do that for myself.

5

MAKING PROMISES

illing out a profile at eHarmony.com embarrassed me, but
the practice of online dating seemed to be a popular thing
to do, and it was clear traditional means weren't doing
much for me, so I clicked around and wrote some things about
myself. I left out my history of drug and alcohol abuse, and
the one-night stands, and I made a promise to myself not to
tell anyone I was looking for love online. If my friends back
home found out I couldn't find a proper date using traditional
methods, I'd be laughed out of town, but I was lonely and it
had become clear to me that I needed a kind of affection my
career couldn't provide.

I scrolled the endless list of profiles belonging to single
women on the website and couldn't help but be taken with a
profile picture of a woman with these strikingly big blue eyes.
I worked up some courage and sent her a request to message
back and forth, which she didn't accept right away. I imagine she

spent that time perusing my own profile, which was not nearly as well done as hers. The best picture I could find of myself featured me with another woman front and center. I thought it was fine because the woman was my sister, but anyone looking at it on the dating website would assume it was probably an ex I might have a hard time getting over. I don't know why Ashley accepted my invitation to message, but I'm thankful she did.

She sent me her phone number and I could barely sit in my cubicle because I was so excited to call her. I stopped by the liquor store on the way home and bought myself a bottle of wine. I poured some into a glass to settle my nerves a little, then picked up my phone to call her.

We talked for an hour or more and I said all the embarrassing things a man will find himself saying in an effort to win over the girl he wants in his life. I was pretty sure from the outset that I wanted her in my life. She was less sure about me. To the point that when she agreed to go out to dinner with me, she gave me the address of a place around the corner from her house so I wouldn't know where she lived. I didn't care. I knew I could win her over.

And I got started on that mission by employing the tried and true tactic of taking her to a super romantic...all-you-can-eat meat buffet! It's not as bad as it sounds. Kind of. I mean, it was a Brazilian steakhouse, which I think shows a little class. It could've been worse. It could have been a Golden Corral or a Ryan's or something. It's not my fault Ashley doesn't appreciate a good buffet.

Of course, I didn't know she didn't like them at the time. Just like she didn't know I couldn't stand lapdogs. In all seriousness, I had a personal policy to immediately end a relationship with a woman once I discovered she owned a lapdog of any kind. But the first time I met Chloe and Sadie, Ashley's yorkie and bischon, respectively (she had two lapdogs!), I baby-talked to them while they licked my face and I pretended to enjoy it, just like Ashley pretended to enjoy the buffet I took her to.

I've learned not to take Ashley to buffets, but I've also come to terms with living with lapdogs. Love requires sacrifice and compromise, but if I've learned anything by getting to be with Ashley, I've learned that the sacrifice and compromise I've given her is worth the patience and tolerance she's given me. (And if you can keep a secret, I'll tell you I still think I'm getting the better end of the deal.)

We connected after dating only a couple of weeks—I know because I felt that tug on my heart. It wasn't long before I knew I wanted to marry her. But it also wasn't long before she could tell I had some baggage, even if she didn't know exactly what kind of baggage—a suitcase full of the masks I had taught myself to wear so well that I kept in my closet. I wore those masks when I pushed myself to the limit with work or drugs and alcohol, or the one I wore when I'd try to go home with the prettiest girl I could find in whatever town I happened to be in that night. Ashley knew I hated my job, but I don't think she understood the complications behind it, that I had some serious self-work to put in.

Meeting her gave me a chance to see my career from a new perspective. I had given my entire professional life to doing whatever it took to climb the corporate ladder and I'd learned a little bit about what I was capable of. I knew I could do it without the help of the people I didn't like working with, and I could certainly do it without the corporate world micromanaging me. My relationship with Ashley had restored my confidence in myself to be the Cole Rodgers I knew I was.

But in true Cole Rodgers fashion, after experiencing success, I did my best to sabotage myself—in this case, that meant leaving Ashley. It's not that I wanted to leave her, but North Carolina was her home, and my dad had an in for me on a job at an insurance consulting firm back in Arkansas. It was something I knew I'd be good at, and it would give me the kind of professional freedom I needed. I told Ashley I was going for a visit, but in reality I went back for a job interview.

"We need to talk," I told her after I accepted the job. She may not have known the details, but she knew I was leaving her in some capacity. Even though I wasn't breaking up with her, I knew I was breaking Ashley's heart, and I didn't like it.

"No matter what," I said to her, "we'll make it work."

She nodded in understanding, but I'm not sure how much assurance she found in my words. Looking back, I probably should've told Ashley I wasn't just going back for a visit, but then again, who knows how she would have reacted had I told her the truth before I had the job. I'm glad things happened the way they did because I'm happy with where we are now, and perhaps another route wouldn't have led to here.

Two weeks after I accepted the job, I sat behind the wheel of a rented U-Haul truck, looking at Ashley in the driver's sideview mirror. I could see her crying as I pulled away and I promised myself that I would go back to Arkansas and succeed because that's what would bring Ashley back to me. That's what would save my damsel in distress.

6

KEEPING PROMISES

I earned my success in my new position at the consultancy firm in Arkansas, and after about eight months of living apart, Ashley joined me in Little Rock, just like I'd hoped. Six months later, we were prepared to get married. We chose to have a ceremony in Wilmington, North Carolina so her family would be close, but we also accommodated my family by getting married in a Catholic Church—we understood that marriage would be a compromise from the beginning, I guess. It was a beautiful church for a beautiful bride, and we were surrounded by the people we love.

What Ashley didn't know at the time was that her groom had spent the last year reviving some old self-sabotaging habits. For example, after the rehearsal dinner, when the bride and her bridesmaids all settled in for a good rest, the groom thought to himself in somewhat of a panic, "Holy shit, I'm about to get married!" It was everything I wanted, but I didn't know how to deal with getting what I wanted at that time.

I feel like lots of grooms have that feeling, but some grooms probably react in the extreme, and I am one of those grooms. My groomsmen followed my lead as the lot of us proceeded to get absolutely slammed. We found a bar and burned the place down, figuratively speaking. I took what seemed like handfuls of Adderall until my heart practically beat out of my chest. I couldn't slow it down. After the bar closed, I found Ashley's room and walked in and sat on the edge of her bed, even though I knew it was bad luck to see the bride on her wedding day—which at some point, the wedding eve had in fact transitioned into the wedding day.

Ashley started her wedding day with lots of tears as she realized how drunk I was, sitting on the edge of her bed and blathering on about one thing or another. I promised her I'd go to my room and get some sleep, but no one would have been able to sleep with that much Adderall in their system, so I stayed up and cranked out some emails for work. By the time the sun came up on my wedding day, I had to take another Adderall just to keep going because I was so hungover.

In the end, we survived it and our wedding was an amazing day—pure bliss—but the man Ashley married that day was a self-centered egomaniac, a narcissist, who was struggling more than she could have ever known, because he was hiding behind a mask that even he couldn't see beyond. By that time, I'd learn to hide my true self so well from everyone that I could even hide from myself. That's not to say I don't have fantastic memories from that time and that day, but I wasn't living an authentic life.

We honeymooned in Costa Rica and I think Ashley and I both found out really quickly that I didn't know how to be married. The realities of the institution itself didn't fit into the idea

I had of it. I thought a married relationship revolved around sex, and we had a lot of it on our honeymoon, until her time of the month showed up and brought us to a halt. I suggested that if we weren't going to have sex, Ashley should provide another favor because I was her husband and this was our honeymoon, dammit! But whether we were married or not, she didn't want to. I was so insecure with myself that I just walked the fuck out to go find a bar, leaving my new wife (whom I'd just sworn to stand by no matter what) crying alone in the fucking shower.

That's not who I am, but it's who I thought I needed to pretend to be at the time. I brought a lot of shit into our marriage and Ashley didn't deserve to have to carry it alone, but she certainly did.

Nine months after we came home from Costa Rica, we welcomed Ava Madison into the world. Less than a year after that, we were pregnant again. And somewhere around that time, I tore my Achilles tendon and couldn't maneuver well enough to make my sales calls, which meant my commission-based job that our single-income family depended on at the time, brought in nothing for a while.

Marriage is hard, especially when tested by things like children, physical adversity, and loss of income, but it's especially hard when you never really gave yourself the time to get to know your significant other before you're forced to endure these tests. Ashley and I moved so quickly in our relationship, and we spent so much of that time apart, that the shimmer on each of us hadn't quite worn off for the other yet when we got engaged. It wore off in a hurry when the going got tough during those first three or four years of marriage—what I like to refer to now as "the messy middle," but I'm proud that we stuck it out. As the duration of our marriage grows longer, I'm sure we'll find ourselves in another messy middle, but I also know we have the power to stick it out again when that day comes. And we have the experience and new mental tools to help us recognize it more quickly and deal with it more effectively.

Inside each of us lives a wise advocate, a just mentor—our internal self—to whom we must listen when only we can hear him. Sometimes you'll have so much shit going on that you can barely hear him, but if you take the time to listen and be vulnerable, he will be there, tugging at your soul when you get out of the shower, or when you put your suit on, or when you give your wife a kiss before you leave the house, or when you walk out into the street to go do whatever it is that you do. You can convince everyone around you that you've got your shit together and you can even convince yourself you've got your shit together, but that's easy because no one can lie to you like you can. If you look hard enough into the mirror, you'll be able to see that you've been feeding yourself a constant stream of bullshit and calling it caviar. If you don't face that fear, if you're too scared to own what's really going on in your life, then you will unconsciously create ways to compound your problems until all of the sudden, everything that you were scared of losing will be lost.

I know because I've lived it. I'm forever indebted to JC, my former therapist, for helping me see through the mask I have a tendency to put on from time to time. Notice I'm writing in the present tense there. That's not a typo. Even though I am light-years away from the wholly self-centered man that Ashley married those years ago, I still struggle with bad habits and self-sabotage when I get complacent. I don't believe it's possible to completely eradicate the closet full of masks we develop in our lives, but I do believe it's possible to fight it, and I also believe we have a responsibility to ourselves and our loved ones to fight it with all we've got.

Unfortunately, there is a stigma associated with getting help, and that's especially true for men. It all goes back to that John Wayne, James Bond, and Clint Eastwood stereotype we feel like we have to strive for. Those guys never went to therapy, but if you think about all the traumatic situations their characters endured on the big screen, they probably need therapy more than anyone. That's not real life, though, and our lives exists in reality, so we have to start improving our own lives by accepting that fact. They're fun heroes to have when we're little boys, but as we grow into men, we should mature and recognize that there are plenty of real-life heroes for us to look up to.

For me, a lot of those real-life heroes wear (or wore) a United States military uniform, like JC. When he served in the United States Marine Corps, one of the first things he and all the other recruits learned at boot camp was the importance of his weapon. Not even the Corps—one of the toughest organizations on this planet—would ask a man or woman to march into battle without the aid of a weapon, and so recruits are issued Kevlar and a rifle and they are trained incessantly in survival skills and battle-field tactics. It's the same thing on the homefront. Just as the Corps equips its recruits for war, we too must equip ourselves for the fight against the masks we wear. We must be broken down in order to be built back up in the image that will serve our cause best.

While I don't have JC's education or expertise as a therapist, I do think it's important that I do all I can to help other men avoid the pitfalls of wearing the masks like I did, and so let me tell you this now: Life is a test. Manhood is a test. Marriage is a test. Parenthood is a test. Leadership is a test. *Everything* is a test. So many men feel they are not worthy of what they have because they don't measure up to some unrealistic idea of a hero. Too many of us in this world are crippled with self-doubt, lack of confidence, and even a victim mindset. Too many of us make excuses for the things we do not accomplish in life. We make too many excuses for why we don't want the ball at the end of the game.

I wanted to find a way to tell men that if they want to better their lives, they have to choose it. They have to ask for the ball. They have to seek out the hard and embrace the struggle. They have to understand that everything is a test, and that these tests are not open-book. They can choose comfort for their lives, but that will make them soft and eager for a short-cut, which will eventually cause them to go dig the masks out of the closet. In the end, I want to assure men that if they can truly man the fuck up and choose themselves—their being, their business, their body, their family—then they'll be able to design their own lives, rather than having someone else, or some*thing* else, design it for them.

The way I have found to tell as many men as possible and have them not only hear what I'm saying, but also embrace what I'm saying, is through the School of Man.

PART TWO
SCHOOL OF MAN

7

WHAT IF?

I'd considered going to graduate school about a year and a half before JC told me I needed to unfuck myself, but instead of getting more formal education and paying a college to teach me something out of a business book, I decided to get a master's degree in real life business. Fitness and working out had always been a passion of mine, so I bought an old CrossFit gym. I wanted my gym to be about more than physical fitness, though. I wanted to help people to break through all kinds of barriers, and I wanted to life-coach them through it.

I created something called Strongwill Consulting and pitched it as executive coaching, but pouring myself into the project allowed me to learn about myself as much as it allowed me to the teach the clients I had begun developing. Part of that is because all good teachers learn from their students, but the other part of that was because I believe in self-discovery. I was doing all I could to learn to be a better leader, to be a better sales trainer, to be a better public speaker. I journaled a lot and eventually compiled a lot of the information I'd gathered and written about into a book called "Energize: Seven Ways to Recharge Your Life." I said I was doing all I could, but of course, just when you think you're doing everything, life reminds you that there's more.

My reminder came when I was mentoring a young man and he made a mistake, and even though I knew—especially as a life coach—that we all make mistakes, it got to me. It pissed me off. That he could make such a rookie mistake after all I thought I'd taught him, set me off. And the mistake was so insignificant that I can't even remember what it was anymore.

But I looked at him and basically said, "What the fuck?" and I just tore his ass up and down. He was 21 years old at the time, and I was supposed to be this seasoned mentor, but I reacted with a primary emotion fueled by absolute anger. And if I'm being honest, that was probably my modus operandi at the time—if someone didn't do things my way, I took it as an attack on what I was trying to build and then BOOM! It was like striking a match at the gas pump. His doing something that didn't align with the goals we'd set forth made me so angry that I lost control of myself and in a way, it was the last straw before I knew I needed to make a major shift.

My mind lives in this state of anxiety that causes me to constantly ask myself "What if...? What if...? What if...?" and at the time I was not in a good place with my physical fitness. It's not that I thought I should be a CrossFit god or anything, but I do believe physical well-being plays a large part in our mental well-being. I knew I needed to make a change already, but then I picked up a copy of the book "The Way of the SEAL: Think

Like an Elite Warrior to Lead and Succeed" by Mark Divine, who also runs a company called SEALFIT. It's a phenomenal company and Mark's a phenomenal guy. He's an ex-Navy SEAL commander willing to teach civilians the fundamentals of what it takes to be a strong leader in the way he learned it from the most elite corps of warriors in the world.

I read the book and it spoke to me in ways I needed to hear at that point of my life. I'm not going to give the meat of the book away, but here's what the book says it will teach you to do:

- *Lead from the front, so that others will want to work for you*

- *Practice front-sight focus, the radical ability to focus on one thing until victory is achieved*

- *Think offense, all the time, to eradicate fear and indecisiveness*

- *Smash the box and be an unconventional thinker so you're never thrown off-guard by chaotic conditions*

- *Access your intuition so you can make "hard right" decisions*

- *Achieve twenty times more than you think you can*

It made a positive impression and a lasting impact on me. The book became the catalyst for developing some better habits in my life. I started meditating and journaling and working on curbing my negative self-talk, and I could see the positive results when I looked in the mirror. Not just physical results, but I could tell I was in a better mental state. I felt good, and I looked good. Like I said before, I like going all in on something good when I find it. I wanted more of what Divine had to offer, so I looked into his company.

SEALFIT offered what they call the Unbeatable Mind Academy—a three day live-in program based on the Navy SEAL's infamous Hell Week. I still had what I like to think of as a "Southern boy" mentality at the time—I was raised in the Bible Belt—so I was a little skeptical of the meditation and journaling and all that kind of woo woo hippy stuff. And on top of that here was this holistic version of warrior stuff out in San Diego, California, the kind of place people where I grew up thought of as the land of fruits and nuts. But I was open to adventure if it meant I could prolong or maybe intensify how good I felt when I looked in the mirror, so I signed up for the retreat, I packed my sneakers, and I got on a plane bound for the West Coast.

When those Unbeatable Mind coaches took us out to do PT (physical training), we started running to the beach, and I thought I was hot shit. I'd gotten my sneakers from Target, I think, and they weren't for running as much as they were for looks. After the first mile, I thought I was going to die.

They made us do step-ups all the way up to the beach, and there were a lot of steps, especially in those Target tennis shoes, and when we finally got to the beach, they made us hold a four-minute plank. A four-minute plank was tough as shit for me, and when I started to give up, I looked over and saw this other guy in the program, Brandon Hayes. He was 42 years old, accomplished triathlete, accomplished financial advisor, super athletic—absolutely jacked. When I started struggling with that plank, I looked over at Brandon and met his eyes. He had a fire in them and he could tell I was breaking down. I was losing it.

"Come on, motherfucker," he said.

I knew right then I liked him. I kept getting back up over and over because Brandon was yelling at me to. That's what teamwork will do for you. And when we finished, we all yelled "Hoo yah!" and ran into the ocean. We got wet, then rolled around on the beach and got sandy, then got wet again and sandy again. Brandon and I got to know each other over the course of the rest of the academy and even though it was a new relationship, I knew immediately that it was an important one for me. Thirty men entered into that academy with me, but only nine of us made it through graduation and Brandon is part of the reason I was among that number.

I liked him because he lifted me up when I was down, but I also discovered I liked him because despite his rock-solid appearance, despite how tough he was, physically and mentally, he knew how to be vulnerable. Brandon was not only a triathlete, he was a recovering alcoholic who'd bared his soul in Alcoholics Anonymous meetings in front of relative strangers. I admired that and could see the burden it had lifted for Brandon.

When I got home from Unbeatable Mind, I was on a natural high and knew I wanted to carry that with me, but beyond that, I wanted to spread it to other men. Not just the bonding elements acquired through strenuous physical adversity, but also through the ability to be vulnerable. We need both of those in our lives if we're going to ultimately meet the demands society places on us and be successful.

Brandon and I have continued to keep up with each other's journey and let me tell you that when I get that text message or call from him that says something to the effect of "Hey man, I'm proud of you," it gives me chills. And I assume it always will because it's coming from a guy who understands the experiences I've been through, from a guy who has shared his own experiences with me. I needed to build that kind of relationship with other men at home.

8

ADAM

I had met a guy named Adam Pratt while I was training up to go to San Diego. He had been a member of the gym I bought, but at the time that I bought it, Adam had stopped working out. When he came back to the gym after a three- or four-month-long hiatus, he found me there working out as hard as I could go to prepare for the Kokoro. Adam showed up to work out at the gym around 5:45am, and by that time I was done with my Murph and moving on to other things.

For those unfamiliar, "Murph" is a workout named after Navy SEAL Lieutenant Michael Murphy, who was awarded the Medal of Honor for his actions during the War in Afghanistan. He earned a lot of medals and when he was killed in action in 2005, he left behind a legacy for a lot of people in a lot of different circles, but I'd argue one of the most inspiring and challenging legacies is his favorite workout, which consists of:

- ▸ One-Mile Run
- ▸ 100 Pull-Ups
- ▸ 200 Push-Ups
- ▸ 300 Air Squats
- ▸ One-Mile Run

A lot of gyms will make it their workout of the day on Memorial Day, but since I was training for what I knew would be the most physically demanding experience of my life, I tried to complete a Murph as often as I could.

The workout's hard and it taxes your mind, but Adam began coming over to me while I was doing my workouts and he started rooting me on. That level of encouragement from another guy who was also putting in some work made the training easier, and what's more, Adam became emotionally invested in my journey, even if he did think my ambitions to conquer a civilian version of SEAL training made me insane. When I got to the Kokoro, Adam followed along as much as he could by watching the videos of my experience he could find on social media.

And when I returned from San Diego, Adam was one of the first people who told me how proud of me he was for setting a goal and accomplishing it. He was there to listen to me when I told him about all I'd learned from the experience and all I'd suffered. I could tell him about my swim buddy losing his life. Not all men are okay with another man opening up emotionally like Adam was, but they should be. We are warriors, but it takes some serious strength to open yourself up to other men and to let other men open themselves up to you, and the Unbeatable Mind taught me that. I also recognized in Adam that he had something special going on. He had the drive and the willingness to connect with himself and to connect with other men.

So when Adam expressed a desire to train for Unbeatable Mind himself—despite having just heard about my classmate not surviving the program—I knew I had a responsibility to help him achieve that.

Adam had a wife and four children, but he'd reached a point where his life had become stale. He felt like he was going through the motions of existence. That's not a negative reflection on his family, and that's important to note. It's just a fact of life that sometimes things can get stale, no matter how happy you are. When you're working from sun up to sun down at a job you aren't passionate about and your wife is shuffling four kids to and from three different schools, when you've got two different kids on two different baseball teams at two different parks—at some point you and your wife are ships passing in the night. These family strains and responsibilities can make life seem stale.

We are meant to be challenged by life, but we don't want to be boxed in by the parameters life has a tendency to put on us. Men are meant to battle, and sometimes when there is no war, our warrior spirit will atrophy. It wears on our psyche until we create unnecessary battles for ourselves, just like I did in my life when I would sabotage myself after I'd given all I had in the name of achievement.

I trained hard for the Kokoro and I knew Adam had a lot of work to put in if he was going to complete the course.

"Before you decide to do this," I told him, "I need you to think long and hard about how far you're willing to push yourself. You're going to have to be all in, if you decide to do it."

When you have a family, you can't set those kinds of priorities by yourself. You need to work through those decisions with your partner, so that's what Adam did. He asked me and Ashley to come talk to him and his wife. We could answer their questions and alleviate their concerns because we'd been through it together already. Ashley was there when Kirk passed away. Ashley knew better than I did what it would take to play that supportive role that would be required by Adam's wife. She knew the sacrifices of having to pick up the parenting slack not just while Adam would be in San Diego, but also while he got his body prepared to withstand that level of physical stress.

During that conversation, Ashley and I talked about how hard the process had been, but also how it changed me for the better. The experience made me a better man who could live a better life, and ripple effects of that in the lives of those around me made it all worth it for everyone. Adam's wife had been a fitness trainer at various gyms, so she understood his desire to physically push himself, and she also has an achiever's mentality. She knows what it means to set a goal and have to put the blinders on to reach that goal.

A few days later, Adam came to me and said, "Man, I don't want to do this, but I feel like I have to." He said he needed something serious to get him serious about doing life. He was at a place where he knew he was going to have to take a chance if he wanted to give his life some purpose—if he wanted to discover the *Why* that could be the engine of his life moving forward.

On the day Adam walked in to begin his training, he was mentally prepared to hit the gym, to test his endurance and strength. As men, as warriors, those physical demands are the first things we think of when we think about improving ourselves. But perhaps it shouldn't be.

That's why that first day, I handed Adam a three-ringed binder with a curriculum inside. Even if he didn't vocalize the words, his face said, "Cole, what the fuck is this?"

The tests he would face at the Kokoro would be about more than just physical ability and we needed to mentally prepare him for that. We practiced some meditative techniques—breathing and visualization exercises. A lot of people—especially here in the South, where masculinity can be especially scrutinized—think it's weird that two guys would isolate themselves at a gym and close their eyes together to simply be present, but there are some basic principles at play in those exercises that help tremendously during other tests down the road. A strong mind can save a weakened body.

I love getting people out of their comfort zones, and I got Adam out of his by telling him to visualize himself at a funeral. I told him to see himself in his Sunday best, to see himself going to church and seeing all the mourners present, mourners who are people he knows well, who care about him. I told him to look into the casket near the altar and when he does, I want him to visualize that the person in that casket is him. His family is on the front row at this funeral and they are all crying. For him. For the absence of his life in theirs.

The exercise was meant to test Adam's vulnerability, to see how far we needed to go in our training, but to Adam's credit, he already knew how to be more vulnerable than most men. In imagining his own funeral, Adam stood there, leaning against the wall there in the gym, surrounded by the sounds of huffing and puffing and weights hitting the floor, but despite his environment, tears ran down his face.

Adam has had a lifelong commitment to being true to himself. His father was a church pastor and Adam spent his childhood watching first-hand how members of his father's congregation behaved in one manner while at church and another manner amongst regular society. That hypocritical nature led him to place a hyper-importance on being the same person, no matter his environment. If he was vulnerable at home, he forced himself to be vulnerable in public. If he is sad, he will cry. If he is happy, he'll laugh. If he's angry, he'll punch something. Adam is committed to being who he is no matter who he is around, and I admire him greatly for that. But just because a person is comfortable being vulnerable, it doesn't mean there isn't more work to put in.

We kept it up. Adam and I started our days with meditation and visualization exercises, and only after we'd cleared our minds did we work on our physical bodies by working out together at the gym. We took both aspects seriously and we hit them hard.

People noticed. Other guys in the gym saw what we were doing. Let me rephrase that: Other guys in the gym saw that we were doing *something*, but they didn't know exactly what. They could tell Adam and I had an intensity about our workouts and about the space that existed between us. They saw the fire we had and they wanted it. When they asked what we were doing, instead of trying to explain ourselves, we answered with, "Come find out."

Of course those guys who showed up willing to actually find out got hit—like Adam—with something they weren't expecting.

They thought we'd put dumbells in their hands and they could workout with us and we'd give them a series of exercises that would probably be tough, but they could do them and they'd have a sense of satisfaction about themselves because of it, and then they'd go about their regular days. Instead, we put a three-ring binder in their hands and had them join us for our meditations and visualizations. That surprised look on their faces will forever bring me joy.

When I think about the origin of School of Man, I can never pinpoint it, but it was some time during this period, when Adam and I had been working out together and other men found themselves instinctively drawn to our connection, our passion, and our intensity.

9

ZACK

"We're doing a hundred rope climbs tomorrow," I said to Adam over the phone.

"Combined?" he asked.

"No," I said. "Each."

"You have got to be kidding me."

I knew that many rope climbs would push us to the limit, but what bothered me was that Adam didn't think he'd be able to do it—I could hear it in his voice. Part of what a brotherhood like ours if for is to always be pushing each other further, and to encourage each other to grow—emotionally and physically, so I pushed him and I depended on him to push me.

The work was hard and it hurt, but Adam and I spurred each other on and together we each knocked out the 100 rope climbs. A couple of the other guys joined us, one of whom had only done seven rope climbs in his life before that day. By the time he walked out of the gym he held his head high after having done 25.

Seeing peers achieve gave me a rush, and seeing them accomplish what they didn't think was even possible gave me a serious high, but unlike the highs of my past, this one was healthy for me, and for those around me. School of Man hatched as a result of one of the healthiest personal and interpersonal times of my life. It feels like there's no other way but for something positive to be had from something born in those circumstances.

Following those initial workouts with Adam and the other guys, I knew I needed to organize the entity that was our group, and I only wanted to include someone in our organization if they were willing to put in the work with the same intensity as we had been. Adam and I vetted them as best we could. We sat down with them and made sure they understood they'd be expected to work on themselves emotionally as well as physically. We told them about learning how to breathe, about being okay with seeing the "negative" parts of themselves and turning those into opportunities to grow as a person, to grow as men. Even hearing those words made some men uncomfortable and they said some various of the phrase, "I don't think this is for me," or "I just want to work out with you guys." But I knew from the outset that School of Man would never be the kind of organization where guys could just work out together and not be a part of each other's lives until they were back in the gym. It had to be something more. In that way, a lot of potential candidates made it easy on us and they weeded themselves out.

But then there are the ones who said they did want to do the work. How do we vet those guys? There's a bit of a catch 22 in that situation because it's nearly impossible to determine who will actually put in the work and who won't until you start putting in the work. Even people you think you know well—when the rubber meets the road you may discover you don't know how much heart they have.

A guy I went to college with named Zack found me on the Internet in one way or another and reached out to me because he'd seen I was doing what would probably be perceived as some self-care. Zack had served his country as an Army medic, but he'd been out of the military for a bit. He sent me a message and told me he knew he also needed to do some self-care because he had made some bad decisions and was fighting some demons in his life. So we met and I told him the kind of work we were doing at School of Man. I told him if he signed on with us we'd force him to take a look in the mirror, so if he was afraid of looking in the mirror, he need not pretend to want to get in on what we had going. He assured me and Adam that he knew what he was getting into and he could handle the work at the intensity we promised to bring. So we told him to meet us at the gym the next morning.

I didn't really have a plan for how to test his physical fortitude, so I asked Adam what we should do.

"Let's put him on the rower," Adam said. "Let's not say a word to him and just put him on a rower."

I agreed, so that's what we did. Zack walked in the next morning and we didn't say a word to him. We just walked him over to the rower and made him start rowing. By that time Jeff had joined us full-time, and the three of us stood behind Zack and watched him row. We didn't talk to him and we didn't talk to each other. We just watched while he pulled. We wanted to see his fight, to see what he had in him, to see what he'd do when he felt under the gun and all alone. When he showed fatigue, when he got gassed, only then did we step right up next to him and say something.

"You've got more," we said. "Let's go." Deep down we wanted to encourage him, but we didn't want it to sound like encouragement that day, so we spoke sternly, with authority. He hadn't earned our friendship yet. We wanted him to feel like he had to keep going, to not hold anything back. It's that desire to hold something back we wanted to flush out, no matter how deep it resided, if it was there.

"Alright, pop off," we told him. "Now you're going to do wall balls. Ten minutes of wall balls."

Zack was hurting, but we could tell he had some fight in him. He stood up and I could tell he was invigorated, but of course, he'd never done wall balls before a day in his life. He thought 10 minutes? No problem. He took the weighted medicine ball in both hands and tossed it against the wall a few feet over his head in front of him, then he'd catch it and squat down. As he'd use his legs to thrust back up, he'd throw the ball again. Over and over and over. But 20 seconds into it, anyone watching could tell that it was going to be a problem. His throws got sloppy. His leg muscles turned to Jell-O. When he wanted to rest, we told him he couldn't put the ball down. When you're spent like that—even standing still—holding a weighted medicine ball can be exhausting.

We took him off the wall balls and made him run with the thought that he had to be about to throw in the towel. But he didn't. Even after he vomited, he kept running. He ran a little, then puked a little, then ran a little more. Me and the other two guys, we're looking at each other like, "Who the fuck is this guy?" because he just wouldn't quit.

When we finally circled back to our starting point and stopped running, Zack broke. But not because he quit. Because he had *not* quit. Because we gave him a chance to see himself again, to see the warrior he was, regardless of the bullshit. He cried and we hugged him and he said, "I need this in my life."

That day with Zack really showed me the potential that School of Man could have for guys who needed virtue as a brotherhood. Zack was on fire that day and he was in a bad way when he first walked through the doors, but his life has skyrocketed since then. He's living right and it's paying off for him. And he's still the most on-fire guy we've got.

10

McPike

Not all of our School of Man participants can just walk in and get put on the rower, though. While we're based in Little Rock, Arkansas, we have some guys who join us remotely. We call them our virtual boat crew and their experience may be slightly different, but it's no less intense. If anything, it means they have to work harder to meet the same standard our in-person crew has to meet. It means they have to be more self-disciplined because they have to be their own accountability partner most of the time. Our in-person crew meets every morning at the headquarters to perform the day's workout, but our virtual boat crew can push that workout to later in the day because there's no one there waiting on them.

Remember Adam McPike from the beginning of the book who saw the two guys carrying the log? He was bouncing back and forth between his life in Little Rock and Northwest Arkansas, so he couldn't meet in person all the time. Adam was basically a hybrid crew member because he'd come to the gym when he was in Little Rock, but he was virtual the other half the time. The good thing is—and what Adam helps prove—is that it doesn't matter what your situation is; if you want to put in the work, you're going to find a way to put in the work to make mental, physical, and emotional growth happen for yourself. It took a serious commitment from him to complete the workouts sometimes. When some of the guys would complain about not having time to complete the exercises, I promise you they got no sympathy from Adam. He would do flutter kicks in his driveway by himself on a Saturday afternoon while his daughter sprayed him in the face with his garden hose. It'd be easy to simply tell her to stop, but he didn't because he knew he'd only be cheating himself. And also, I think his daughter probably thought it was a hell of a lot of fun.

"You've just got to get it in when you can get it in," he told me. "It's got to be a priority if it's going to get done."

Another benefit of being in the virtual boat crew that at least one of our guys—Rob—would consider me remiss if I didn't mention it; our remote guys don't have to clean the bathrooms.

We had an occasion where virtual boat crew member Rob—we'll talk more about him later—came to Little Rock and participated in the daily workouts for a while. The first day, we sweat it out, then he headed toward the door to leave before one of our local guys, Doc, asked him to grab the cleaning supplies.

"What?" Rob asked.

"Yeah, we clean the bathrooms," Doc said.

"What the hell, man?" Rob said. "I'm not in the Navy anymore. I don't clean bathrooms."

"Well, we clean 'em here," Doc said. "Grab this freakin' mop and let's go."

11

IVERSON

nother of our virtual boat crew guys is Phillip Iverson. He lives in the central part of Washington state and works a job doing background checks for a human resources department. He and his wife moved from California to Washington with a plan to stay there three to five years, but nearly a decade later, they're still there. When Phillip sat down at the end of the year to lay out his goals for the coming year, he realized he ended up in a rut that didn't have him excited about life. He needed that excitement and some direction. He clicked around on the Internet and found a class we were doing at the time called Apex. As part of the class, we jumped on a Zoom call every day for the first 10 consecutive days of the year and discussed setting goals to optimize personal performance in various aspect of life.

I listened to Phillip and it became clear to me that he needed more than a 10-day Zoom call. And that's not a reflection of some shortcoming in Phillip; if anything, it's a testament to

Phillip's ability to recognize a void within himself and to go do something about it. A lot of people don't recognize the need and try to fill that void with all kinds of unhealthy things—and my own history is living proof of that.

Phillip needed better goals, yes, but he needed more than that. He needed to connect with other men. His wife had girlfriends she hung out with regularly and he saw the enjoyment she got out of that time with them. She and her friends discussed real issues in their lives and processed them together. She bonded with them.

Phillip had men in his life that he saw at work and church and around the neighborhood, and they'd see each other and shake hands and one would ask, "How are you doing?" and the other would undoubtedly always say something to the effect of "fine" when in actuality they might both be anything but. He didn't have the kinds of friends he could confide in. He wasn't doing life with any other men, and that makes doing life harder. I told Phillip I thought he might get something out of School of Man and I sent him some links to check out.

Most men come to us because they're attracted to the physical challenge—they march willingly toward the gym because they know they're going to get in shape and everyone around them will be able to see the results of the work they're putting in. The internal, emotional stuff, they aren't as eager to take on. Phillip was the opposite. The physical component of the curriculum did not appeal to him at all, but he wanted to develop meaningful connections with other men through the emotional work the class would require. As he put it, he didn't have much desire to "play G.I. Joe" with us, but if it would bring him the male connections he was missing, he agreed to give the School of Man a try.

I'm not going to say Phillip entered into the School of Man reluctantly, but he clearly held something back. When he explained to his wife that he was going to give us a go, he broke a cardinal rule about what we stand for: He wasn't honest and up-front with her.

Phillip had previously tried to fill the void of male bonding in his life with things that could never have accomplished that task, and because of that bad decision, he was doing positive work in a 12-step recovery program, which had been successful. He told his wife School of Man would be another outlet, a sort of continuation and supplement to his 12-step program. He told her he and a bunch of other guys were going to read some books and have a call once a week, which is the most understated, simplistic, and—frankly speaking—laughable explanation I've ever heard applied to School of Man.

He should've told her the truth of it. A significant part of the work we're doing is teaching men how to take off those masks they wear. The masks I wore when I was in Nashville, partying all night and then waking up the next day to be the best employee I could be. By not telling his wife exactly the kind of work he'd be doing, he was learning to wear a new mask, albeit probably one that wasn't much more than a variation of another mask he already knew how to put on well.

Phillip had had male role models growing up. His dad was there when he needed him, but they weren't especially close. When he was in 4th grade, a terrible accident left Phillip's brother with burns over 92% of his body, and that kind of trauma altered the family dynamic. For obvious reasons, his parents showered his brother with attention and it affected Phillip in ways he's still trying to unpack decades later. But there are other factors surrounding what Phillip calls his "daddy issues." If I've learned anything in my life about men, it's that we all have at least some little bit of our own daddy issues, and that they affect us for our entire lives.

Around that same time in Phillip's life, his dad started his own contracting business. Self-employment takes a lot of time and effort, which meant he'd leave early in the morning and get back home late at night. His dad was his pack leader in the Boy Scouts of America, but otherwise, Phillip didn't see his dad much. His dad rarely showed up to watch him participate in sporting events or other extra-curricular activities. It's not that his father was a bad dad; he just wasn't there in all aspects of his life. He needed someone who was dependable, always there for him no matter what the situation.

Phillip found male role models in other places after he grew into adulthood. He looked to a man we'll call Bob for an example of how to be a great businessman. Bob had an impressive business acumen—he was cutthroat—and he was a great father, but he didn't know how to balance those things with his spirituality, which is something that's extremely important to Phillip.

Phillip also had a man we'll call Mark, who is a great spiritual leader, a giant in his home and work with a true servant's mentality—he'd give you the shirt off his back—but you didn't want to follow him into business because sometimes giving away the shirt on your back meant taking a significant financial hit.

But even with having multiple male role models in his life, Phillip never had a closely knit group of male friends. There was never any peer accountability and bonding he could rely on. School of Man aimed to change that.

Because he had had some legitimate injuries to his knee and back, Phillip was working out with a personal trainer a couple of times a week to recover. When he joined Class 004 of School of Man, he supplemented those workouts with a modified version of the School of Man workouts he could do without aggravating his injuries. He read the books geared toward personal growth and development and he participated in the group discussions about the material. He found some of the books to be especially hard-hitting and they forced him to dig deeper to unpack things he wouldn't otherwise have unpacked. The books played a key role in Phillip's growth, but he knew they could only be part of the equation. The other part, the more important part, was that he could process that material in a safe space with guys who were also processing their own. They could discuss the ideas and share their feelings with each other without fear of judgment. If you've never had a group of guys you can trust like that before in your life, suddenly gaining one can be absolutely liberating.

In a relative instant, Phillip had 30-40 men with 30-40 unique viewpoints he could talk to in a variety of settings—as a one-on-one conversation, as a small group, or in an at-large setting. These are guys he could call at all hours of the night to get real, candid opinions and insight on his relationship, his finances, his emotions, his work, his entire life. And he could offer the same in return. That's something a lot of guys don't realize they're bringing to the table when they sign up for something like this, but it's just as important. It's a give and take, and they're an equal part of the equation.

"I realized I can share some of the things with others I took for granted," he told me one day. "Because of my life experiences that I'd previously taken for granted, I have some insights that

I can share with others that could benefit them and what they're going through."

For a person to realize he has talents and gifts that are worth sharing is to instill that person with an invaluable amount of self-confidence. That's what having a brotherhood can do. It's the reason men need each other.

Having interpersonal relationships with other men isn't just about being all kumbaya, it's also about calling someone out on their shit. We need someone we trust to help hold us accountable. When Phillip picks up the phone and calls one of his School of Man peers to vent about something happening in his life, it's up to the guy on the other end of the phone to tell Phillip if he's only making excuses for not facing things head on. It's up to them to say, "Phillip, that sucks, but now shut up and man up and do something about it." Without that accountability, he might throw himself a pity party and never adequately address the actual issue at hand. Without that accountability, he may drift into the bad habit of putting on a mask that feels comfortable. Without that accountability, he won't force himself to grow.

At the end of School of Man, all the hard work and soul searching, all the reps and the sweat, all the bonding and the learning to trust, culminates in what we call The Crucible, which is 55 consecutive hours of hell. We bring in former Navy SEAL training cadre—those who have trained the most dedicated service members in our military—and we turn them loose on our guys to test their physical endurance and their mental fortitude. The cadre put our guys through an absolutely rigorous range of torturous exercises throughout the event. We hose them down with water. We deprive them of sleep. We push their bodies and minds to the limits. It's hell, but it's a hell the class endures together. It's a shared experience meant to test every fiber of a man's being. It's the reason we do those visualizations, so we're able to withstand prolonged physical pain. The Crucible is the hardest thing a lot of these guys will ever do in their lives.

So, how do you explain a desire to subject yourself to something like that to a loved one? To a spouse? Especially when you haven't even told the truth about what School of Man is yet. Phillip's wife thought he was basically in a book club. But even those remote members in the Virtual Boat Crew are required to participate in the Crucible in order to graduate.

"It's going to be a men's retreat," he told her. "Me and a group of guys are basically going to be hanging out and not doing much."

Of course, nothing could be further from the truth. And when Phillip got home and turned to social media to tell his friends about what he'd been through—something that ended up being a series of 24 separate posts—his wife knew something didn't add up about the "men's retreat."

Phillip fundamentally misunderstood the program he'd entered into when he decided to not include his wife in the decision. He thought this whole School of Man thing would solely focused on him—and in a way, I guess it is—but really it's about learning to be who you are all the time, and learning to trust those in your life you need to. By cutting his wife out of the decision-making process, he cheated her and himself from a shared experience and an opportunity for guidance and counseling.

Had he been upfront with her, she could have comforted him as he packed his suitcase with gear and wondered what the hell he had gotten himself into. That comfort is part of the reason we have spousal relationships and Phillip was robbing himself of that benefit. And in the final moments of the Crucible, when all of his classmates were having shared experiences with their loved ones, when they were showered in hugs and kisses and words of affirmation and affection, Phillip didn't get that. That's when he knew without a doubt that he'd made a mistake in not including her in his journey.

He had been afraid to tell his wife that he needed to do School of Man because—among other reasons—he didn't want her to know he wasn't already a warrior. He didn't want to project an image of weakness and vulnerability. He had been so afraid of having a conversation with her that ended with her telling him "no" instead of being willing to accept and embrace that there might be a "yes" involved.

Here's an excerpt from a post Phillip published to social media upon his return:

> Saturday morning my day started off by being told I was dead. I then became a casualty that my group had to contend with for a while. Won't go into detail other than to say I couldn't have asked for better men to take care of me than Brian, Brian, Jeff, Mac Millan Danette (Sean), Scott, Brandon, and Marc. Not sure why I was picked, but part of me thinks it was because I was probably the lightest one in the group weighing in at 160lbs when soaking wet. Either way, I was happy to be in the good hands of great men.
>
> Yet, for some reason the two cadre didn't stop there. No, I distinctly remember Jud continuing to push

me. Mind you all, I was "support" and supposed to be somewhat restricted. Thankfully for me, Jud didn't see it that same way. I'm grateful that he and his fellow cadre pushed me to my "limits". It would have been easy to write me off, but the pushing helped. It showed me where I was stronger than I thought and where I needed to push more. (Yes, I just did thank the person who put me through the wringer for a good portion of the weekend.)

Throughout the morning, I continued to find new ways to push myself and use my voice to encourage and motivate when I didn't think possible. I have always struggled to have meaningful verbal interaction with others (huge lack of self-esteem). While I didn't conquer it that day, I made some significant leaps. Also being told that I had to start looking everyone in the eye and only say "thank you" when being given a compliment helped (thanks Cole).

What I also saw that day in full effect was selfless service. My two brothers in this journey of support Eric and Rob, showed me new ways to give of self for the sake of others. They were always hustling and moving. Never stopping. Finding new ways to show strength and solidarity. They could have taken easy ways out, but they didn't. They set a standard and example for me that I tried to keep up with from that point forward.

> This would be needed as one of my biggest fears (ha
> - never told Cole or Viguerie about this ahead of time)
> was going to happen real soon. I was going to be
> forced to abandon my wallflower tendencies and do
> so rather loudly in public.

Of course, when his wife was reading things like that, she said, "What were you doing in Little Rock at your men's retreat?" She also wanted to know why he didn't tell her what he'd actually gotten involved with.

His rationale at the time, he told her, was that he was doing School of Man for him and he didn't understand why it would impact her. He didn't want her to worry about the physical stress he'd be under with the Crucible.

She was hurt and upset that Phillip hadn't been upfront about School of Man. Of course, she had noticed a change in Phillip, long before the Crucible and the social media posts, but she wasn't sure what to attribute it to. Her husband had developed a deeper self-confidence than he had had before. And understanding what was behind the change, encouraging him to be upfront about School of Man, allowed him even more self-confidence. Once he came clean, she embraced her role in supporting him. That's the kind of trust that makes a marriage work.

Because he left her out of his School of Man experience, he's signed up to do the program all over again, from start to finish. It's not rare for guys to want to do the Crucible again, but Phillip will be the first graduate we've had to complete the entire curriculum again, start to finish. He wants the accountability and treatment that every new class member experiences. He wants his wife to see him work on himself as he's gaining and refreshing the knowledge and tools he's developing to analyze and improve his life, his relationships, his finances, his emotions, and his work. Men sharing feelings is not something our society and our culture does easily, but it's important, and he wants her to see that he can do it.

"The first time around I saw other men who had their wives involved and what it did for their relationships," he told me, "I saw them with their friends and family waiting there for them at the end of the Crucible and I wanted that for me and Julianna. It'll be a unique moment in our relationship and our marriage moving forward."

I think they're both looking forward to that the second time around.

Phillip and Julianna have an adopted son, and Phillip looks forward to passing on what he's learned about himself.

"I want to give him the best that I can," Phillip said. "I've never been overly athletic, never been one to push myself really hard. I've been comfortably content most of my life. I can take what comes at me and succeed, but never really push hard. School of Man made me want to show my son how to push hard. I want to show him that he doesn't need to quit, that he doesn't need to take *no* for an answer. There are things I've done and do now that are uncommon. I want him to have a solid relationship with me and know that he can grow up to be the secure confident young man that I never was. I don't want him to feel ashamed of me or of himself. School of Man broke me down to the basics and rebuilt me so I can move forward in my life as a better father and husband."

School of Man is helping him accomplish those goals. It's giving Phillip that confidence he needs to be the best husband

and father he can be, the one he wants to be. When he returned home after completing the Crucible, and he got back into his routine, he showed up for his regular appointment with his therapist. This is a therapist he'd been talking to on a regular basis for over six years.

"The day after you completed your Crucible," she told him. "You were such a different person that day than I've ever seen before. I could tell that something had made a noticeable impact in your life like nothing else had since we have being doing work. The Crucible has been more defining for you than the loss of your father, the loss of your mother-in-law, moving away from your family; everything. Such a positive impact on you. I'm happy to see you doing it all over again."

Phillip was battling some medical issues the first time he went through the Crucible with Class 004 and because of that, we had to modify his experience a little. As hard as we are on our guys, their safety is always a top priority. We want to push them, but we don't want anybody getting hurt. I think an additional reason Phillip is so eager to through the class again, is to prove to himself that he can do it without any modifications.

I assured him it wasn't necessary to do it again, and that the Crucible he experienced was anything but easy. Even if it was modified, the cadre still made it hard. Regardless, Phillip is going to do it again, and that's evidence already of things he's learned from the program because one of our primary goals is to teach our guys not to let fear control them. To teach them that they can charge toward the most difficult things they're facing, rather than running from them.

12

MAC

nother guy by the name of Sean Mac—we call him Mac—
already had that confidence to run toward difficult things,
especially when it came to physically demanding feats. By
the time he came to School of Man, he had already successfully
completed multiple triathlons, ridden his bicycle across Iowa,
ridden in multiple 100-mile mountain bike races over difficult
terrain, run numerous marathons, and participated in a couple
of events with GORUCK, which builds team-based challenges of
"unknown time and distance, with unknown challenges along
the way." And on top of all that, he's a veteran of the United
States Navy and a registered nurse—two experiences in his life
that require him to run toward the proverbial fire, rather than
away from it.

Mac's sister had known a couple of guys who had gone
through School of Man and because of what she understood
about the Crucible, she thought he might be interested. Indeed,

the same desire he had to pursue his previous extreme sports challenges drew him to School of Man. He filled out our online application and we took a look at how he'd answered our questions to see how serious this guy was about taking on the curriculum.

We dialed him up where he lives in Colorado and I reiterated to him that the physical challenge is not all School of Man is about, and in fact, it's not even the biggest part of what we're about. I gave him some more things to think about, things he should consider before taking this on, and he gave *us* some things to think about before agreeing to take *him* on. A lot of people would think we'd take anybody on that's willing to pay us—that seems like a pretty obvious rule for running a successful business, and I get that—but we're not that kind of business. That's one of the things that make us great—we aren't here to make money as much as we're here to build a brotherhood of men who can rely on each other.

During our interview period, I had several calls with Mac, and I connected him with a few of the guys who had been through the class so they could talk about their experiences. That's one of the best things about the nature of our program—we have a very diverse group of guys who are open to sharing themselves with other men who may be on the cusp of making a needed change and bettering themselves. They share stories of their successes in business, as well as their failures in business. They share their stories of successes and failures in their relationships. They share the reasons for those failures, which are sometimes subtle things and sometimes not so subtle things—addiction to drugs, alcohol, porn; you name it. Those stories made Mac realize he'd taken his career—and he'd had a couple—for granted, and he'd probably also taken his relationships for granted. Even in those first few conversations, he learned to better appreciate what he had, and he desired to be better moving forward.

I ended up having several calls with Mac before we both agreed he should join School of Man class of 004. Given his background in seeking out extreme sporting events, I never had any doubts as to whether or not he could complete the ongoing physical commitment, but even the most fit candidates don't easily adapt to the hardships of the Crucible. And like I said, the physical aspect isn't even the largest part of the transformation for individuals who successfully complete the School of Man.

After he'd been through the program, I asked him how the Crucible compared to the other events he'd done in his life. He gave me such a good answer that I'm not even going to try to summarize it. These are his words nearly a year after he made it through:

Nothing compares to the Crucible. To this day, the Crucible is the hardest thing I've ever done. A lot of those events that I did were difficult—don't get me wrong—and they took a lot of discipline and training and willpower leading up to it and to get through. With the Crucible it wasn't all about me. It was about me, but as much as it was about me, it was about the rest of my team, and the rest of my class as well. I could've gone into the Crucible the most fit I'd been in my entire life, or I could've gone in there the least fit I'd been in my entire life—both would've had impacts far beyond myself.

So many people are so focused on themselves, so enamored with everything they're accomplishing or not accomplishing, that they are neglecting the people around them, and neglecting to acknowledge how they could help them. Nobody's ever going to be perfect—not you, not your parents, not your spouses, not your children or your neighbor or your best friend. We need each other and each of us has to recognize that. It's hard, but it's especially hard for men, I think, because we're trained from the earliest of ages that we don't need anybody else for anything. We're taught that we should be able to take care of ourselves, to walk it off, to get back on the horse. There are some important lessons in learning to get back on the horse, but it's at least as important that we understand we don't have to go it alone. We can get some help to get back on the horse, but we also can't be lazy, and we need to have the fortitude to *want* to get back on it.

The Crucible teaches that. That's a horse that will buck you right the fuck off at the first sign of complacency. It's designed to. But it's also designed to show the benefit of being okay with accepting help, as well as accepting the responsibility to help someone else get back on their horse. What may not be noticeable to outside eye, is that the Crucible is different from other extreme events because it's centered on fostering a team environment.

The fastest any man in the world has ever run a marathon in recorded history is two hours, one minute, thirty-nine seconds, when a Kenyan named Eliud Kipchoge did so in Berlin in 2018. Most men average a time of about four and a half hours. Yes, when you're running a marathon, you're challenging your body, but you've got a lot of time to reflect during those four and a half hours. The same thing's true for endurance mountain bike races, or any other kind of endurance race, for that matter. Lots of time to spend in your head, with your thoughts. Lots of time to recalibrate, adjust fire, adapt, so you can better overcome the obstacles you're facing.

The Crucible isn't like that. There's no time to reflect on what you're overcoming in the midst of overcoming it because something else is waiting on you—just like in life—there is always some unknown that you're running toward when you're already tired, already spent, already out of energy or patience or you are full of doubt about your ability to conquer, or even survive.

The Crucible is a three-day exercise, but preparation for it starts months before. Had Mac done the Crucible out of the gate when he joined us in January of 2019, he wouldn't be connected to the nine other guys who were part of his class. And I don't think he would've been ready to do it for his wife and kids and the rest of his loved ones. He still saw it as something he was doing alone.

I can't tell you everything about what the School of Man experience is like because it's impossible. Any attempt I make in telling you what to expect wouldn't live up to the actual experience, which is why so much of what I'm writing now seems to remain at the surface level. The depth—and the experience is certainly deeper; deeper than most participants have ever gone in their lives—only exists once the bonds have been forged between each class's participants. It's all dependent upon the trust developed between them and the trust that exist between the men and School of Man's leaders. That's why each class starts by having everyone sign a non-disclosure agreement. Such an agreement is necessary at the beginning of the class, but no legal piece of paper could ever be as strong as the trust that exists between our guys once the class is in full swing. Everyone involved understands the power of the trust they put in each other when they're sharing personal vulnerabilities at the highest levels.

We also don't want to share too much about the School of Man curriculum with those not in the program because it might detract from anyone's experience who might go through the program later. But here's something I can share: Each month a School of Man Warrior Box arrives in the mailboxes of our class participants. Inside, they find something built especially for their class at that specific juncture of their training. Sometimes it's something to inspire them, but always something to challenge them. The contents of their Warrior Boxes spark conversations between the men, it gives them a way to relate to each other, to question each other, to share philosophies and experiences. It's the fodder of discussions we have on our Man Up Monday calls, in the text messages bouncing between our guys no matter where they are in the world. In Class 004, we had Mac in Colorado, Phillip in Washington, and other men in the virtual boat crew coming from California and Japan, in addition to our in-person crew going through the class at our headquarters in Little Rock.

No matter where people are, the Warrior Boxes and the conversations they encourage are all about helping our guys discover their *Why*. The reason *why* they are improving themselves, the thing that drives them to change, the motivation behind getting up a little earlier, staying a little later, making sacrifices one ordinarily wouldn't make...unless a good reason *why* exists in their lives. Bruce Wayne watched his parents get murdered in the street by petty thieves and that became his *Why* for a lifetime of bringing justice to criminals throughout Gotham City. He took a negative incident in his life and made something positive out of it. Obviously we can't all have an origin story like Batman—or his superhero budget—but we can make dramatic changes to our lives if we are willing to discover our *Why*.

When Mac joined School of Man, his *Why* started and ended with wanting to be better for his wife, Danette, and their children, Brooke and Kaleb, and the rest of his family. He was approaching School of Man with the same mentality he took to his endurance races—ready to reflect and recalibrate so that he could prove to himself that he could conquer another thing. Something else to say he had dug deep for and prevailed. Something for the betterment of himself, and also for him as a husband and father. But two months into the class, Mac's *Why* also included being better for the nine other guys in his class who knew they could depend on him no matter the time or place. Through constant conversations with his classmates, he realized his *Why* was no longer about him.

That realization happened because he made the conscious decision to trust the process and show his classmates his vulnerabilities. He shared things with the brotherhood he had never even shared with his wife—and they've been happily married for nearly 30 years. The great irony of this kind of thing is that by opening up the part of himself that he's kept locked away, his capacity for bettering himself grew exponentially.

There are a lot of men in our society who have learned to half-ass everything they do, and School of Man is the antidote to that kind of behavior. Mac would put his warrior mask on when he participated in marathons and triathlons and all his other extreme sporting events, and that netted positive results. He planned to do the same thing when he enlisted in the School of Man, but as everyone else in his class began taking off their masks and talking about their vulnerabilities, Mac learned to trust them enough to take his mask off too. When he did, he learned he never needed a warrior mask in the first place because just as a real monster doesn't need a monster mask and a real alien doesn't need an alien mask, a real warrior doesn't need a warrior mask. And Mac is a warrior.

Vulnerability is not weakness. Far from it. Vulnerability in front of other men is strength. But, of course, sharing your vulnerabilities takes trust, and trust is scarce in today's society. Mac's got buddies he can grab a beer with, he can ride his bike with socially, and he can vent to those guys about things in his life, about his relationship with his wife—we all need to vent about our spouse occasionally, right? It doesn't mean we don't love them, because we do, but when you have a partner who is always there, problems are going to arise. That's the nature of the beast. It's also the nature of the beast that we vent about those problems, about our spouse's behavior. There are our friends who will say, "Fuck her, man. That's some shit. She's crazy," because they think that's what we want to hear. They're yes men. No shame in it; we've all been a yes man at someone point in our lives, and probably still are in some circles. But it's also important to have the kinds of buddies who aren't afraid to push back on your behavior, to hold you accountable to your relationships.

When Mac picks up the phone and vents to one of his School of Man classmates, whether they think he's right or wrong, or if they are indifferent, they're more apt to say, "How can we make this better?" or more importantly, "What part of this situation do you own?" There will always be issues that arise in our relationships and in our lives, and it's easy to forget sometimes that we made the bed we're must lie in. We're *always* making the bed we'll eventually lie in. School of Man is a brotherhood that exists to remind its members of that. There's an accountability that probably most closely resembles therapy or counseling, but it's different because it's not one person with an advanced degree holding you accountable, it's a collection of a lot of people from all backgrounds holding you accountable, and they're doing so in a reciprocal environment. They expect you to hold them accountable as well.

Mac traveled to Little Rock for what we were calling our Performance Academy at the time, and it was there he'd meet face-to-face for the first time these guys he'd been conversing with over the phone and the Internet for a couple of months. His mentality leading into that experience was that he had so much time and energy already invested into School of Man that he needed to play the long game of staying healthy for the Crucible, which was coming up two months later. Even if that meant not giving his all during the Performance Academy. He didn't want to get hurt and not be able to experience the fullest intensity he expected during the Crucible, the event that attracted him to School of Man in the first place.

But when he was in Little Rock with his classmates, enveloped by the fraternity he and his brothers had created amongst themselves under the School of Man banner, Mac could feel the bigger mission. He showed up with a priority to not get hurt so he wouldn't jeopardize his ability to complete the Crucible later—the culmination of everything he'd put into the program thus far—but surrounded by the rest of his class, he realized that even if he did get hurt, it wouldn't keep him from coming to the Crucible.

"Even if I get hurt, I'm going to be a part of the team until the end. I'm going to be here to serve these guys in whatever capacity I can," he said.

Despite a potential injury keeping him from physically crossing that finish line himself, he would still want to be there for his classmates emotionally and help them however he was able.

By understanding that he would always be a part of something bigger, that he could always contribute to the team, that this test (re: life) isn't something he has to do on his own, he experienced—and is experiencing—personal growth that can expand into other aspects of his life. Mac will take that same team mentality into his marriage, into his family, and into his professional career. He learned not to hold anything back and live life to the fullest. He learned that by giving his current task his all, he is both showing and earning respect from those around him.

School of Man brings together guys who have always wanted more, even when they're not necessarily in a bad place. Guys who either have a fire inside them, or want one. We instill that kind of drive by providing a playbook and a practice facility that is a proving ground for men who recognize we are all flawed, but who also have the guts to do something about it. Each class is a group of men that teaches each other how to develop and maintain positive relationships they can depend on. That group is a safe environment where they're shown that it's okay to share vulnerabilities and as they continue to practice the skills they learn from School of Man, they carry it into other aspects of their lives. The first outside application of that practice is usually in the relationship our guys have with their spouse or partner.

Our better halves are what help us be the men we are called to be. There would be no School of Man if we didn't have our ladies pushing us to be better men because they know when we as men remove the lid on our growth, our families are directly impacted in a positive way. Ashley moved halfway across the country with me so I could follow a dream. She's indirectly contributing to my dream in too many ways to mention, but she's also directly contributing to my dream by having conversations with other significant others in the School of Man Support Crew. When we sat down with Adam and his wife to talk about embarking on the program to train for Kokoro, I could have talked until I was blue in the face when trying to convince his wife Adam would be okay, but the linchpin was Ashley. She could share what she'd been through, what our family as a whole had been through, and what changes she'd seen in me. Had she not been there, who knows if Adam would have started training, and if he hadn't, who knows if School of Man would've ever happened. My wife's support is crucial when it comes to my involvement in School of Man, just as it is in every other aspect of my life.

Mac avoided the mistake Phillip made by relying on his support crew—his wife Danette—from the outset of his involvement with School of Man. Here's what he had to say about having that support:

> Even with the best of Class 004 support, I wouldn't have gotten through any of it without Danette, to be honest. Whether I was on a call and got off the call emotionally drained either because of something

I had shared, or because I was there for another brother, or after completion of a Warrior Box, she was always there to pick me up, support me. There were a couple of Warrior Boxes near the end that were extreme in nature and she was out in the garage with me, supporting me, holding the video camera for the Zoom call—she was very crucial. And for the Crucible, she came with me, and became the support crew for me and some of the other guys in the virtual boat crew. She got us all up early that morning, got us all to the rendezvous point where we were starting. She was there when we finished, helped us get all our gear loaded...so yeah, my wife was extremely, extremely involved.

The world has an abundance of men who claim to be warriors, but it's rare to find a humble warrior. The School of Man has a knack for humbling men by pushing them to further than they think they can go, buy digging deeper into their emotions and behavior than they have ever dug before. Being humbled is an irreplaceable part of learning to be vulnerable. Mac found himself humbled after approaching the program with a self-focused mentality and then walking away with a team-focused mindset. He knew he had been humbled, Danette knew he had been humbled, so that allowed him to be vulnerable with her and share why he was humbled.

A lot of people see our videos of grown men being yelled at by other grown men and think we're demeaning them because of some power trip, but I assure you that's the poorest of attempts to understand what we're about. We utilize military-style training techniques to humble them in a way that doesn't degrade them. Any closer look to what we're doing, and anyone would be able to see that not only do we not degrade our guys, but we empower them. We partner with current and former military training cadre to ensure we're doing things right. The same guys who have trained Navy SEAL teams are training our guys. They have churned out some of the most driven and successful human beings on this planet. They spent a good portion of their training with grown men in their faces, yelling at them, but I don't think anyone will argue that they've been degraded. This training is not so much about lording cadre power over candidates as it is about understanding what real power is, and then instilling it into our participants.

Most men don't understand that they don't always have to be the tough guy to be worthy of love. They don't always have to be right. That doesn't mean men always have to be wrong, either, but we don't naturally feel okay with being wrong, ever. That makes things hard on a partner, when you aren't ever willing to admit you're wrong. And it also doesn't mean you're a bad person or a bad partner if you don't like admitting your wrong. But our partners and our loved ones deserve for us to recognize that we *might* be wrong. Mac has always been a good guy, a good husband—he's been married to his wife for nearly three decades—a good father, but now he's an even better one.

Right after the Crucible, I asked Danette if she'd seen a change in her husband since he'd been working with School of Man, and she had a great answer.

"I have noticed a change," she said, "but I'll let you know where we are in six months."

Danette's smart enough to recognize that change isn't something that can happen in a short period of time. Real change takes years and decades and sometimes lifetimes of work. Change seems certain, it feels easy to make when you're on an emotional high like Mac was after completing the Crucible, but Danette wanted to see if it would stick after they got home and into their regular life routines. That's when the real work for Mac—and all our brothers—begin.

All we're doing is giving men the resources and the motivation and the community to begin that transformation. We're breaking down their current mindset so they can start anew and more easily live a life they want, free of the stereotypical burdens society has placed on them. Through experiencing humility comes the necessary acceptance of vulnerability. That's part of the reason the guys clean the bathrooms at the gym every day. It's yet another reminder to practice humility.

So, did the lessons Mac learned and the changes he'd made stick? I asked him about a year after he'd finished the Crucible.

"I'm not perfect," he said. "I still struggle every day now, but I will say I'm less quick to point blame, and I'm quicker to accept responsibility. These are things Danette has probably been ready for for many, many years."

Mac has always struggled with the meditations because he has a hard time quieting his mind and he still has a hard time, but he's working at it. And whether he's patient enough to recognize it or not, he's getting better at learning to concentrate on nothing but his breathing and the stillness of his body.

He has learned to make the best of things. He always expected a lot out of himself—sometimes too much—and those expectations have had a tendency to roll over into his expectations for the people around him. Now, he's got the resources to better deal with any disappointment those lofty expectation may beget. He's learning how to be a more well-rounded husband, and in some ways a more well-rounded father.

"I use everything I've learned in the last year to continue trying to live my life in the way I want to," he told me. "I have my slip-ups, but for the most part I stay true to myself. I stay true to our ethos."

SCHOOL OF MAN ETHOS

A Man Is Driven By His Why
A Man driven by "WHY" can bear any "how." He willingly places himself in the fire, knowing he will come out stronger and more tempered. He steps gladly into the discomfort zone in order to define his purpose and share it with the world.

A Man Runs To The Sound Of Adversity
A Man is never afraid of confrontation or conflict, as he understands that is where true growth lies. By running towards the sound of adversity he knows not only will he better himself, but better the situation through his actions.

A Man Commits To Taking Action
A Man designs his path, embraces it, and walks it with pride. He knows that the only easy day was yesterday.

A Man Does Not Make Excuses

A Man takes extreme ownership for his actions as he knows that ownership is the very fabric of integrity of a Man's life.

A Man Chooses Integrity As His Value Of Choice

At the end of the day, all a Man has his word and his name. If he dishonors either of those, he has nothing. Knowing this, Man chooses to be honest with himself, with his team, and those closest to him—he knows dishonesty will lead to erosion of character and legacy in a blink of an eye.

A Man Vows To Renew His One-Second Contract...Daily

A Man is grounded in the present. Understanding that there are only 86,400 seconds in a day, the one-second contract makes him ever-present. He chooses family, adventure, brotherhood, and his purpose to guide him throughout his day. Success is not owned, but only rented.

A Man Is Not A Shitty Teammate

A Man puts the spotlight on the team, before himself. By being a "Team Guy" he takes responsibility for seeing his Brothers succeed at the highest level, and helps propel them to heights they have never experienced before.

A Man Is A Servant Leader

A Man is willing to teach and share his experiences with others, including his failures. He passes on what was imprinted on him so that others can succeed at the highest level.

A Man Embraces Change

A Man is flexible in design. He embraces living a life full of vision and accepts that all things change for a reason

A Man Embraces Legacy

A Man knows his greatest gift on this earth is to leave a legacy full of impact. Always pursuing self-mastery, Man embodies the "Warrior" mentality and strives to impact as many lives as he can while on this earth.

13

RICK

Rick Pena lived in Milwaukee, Wisconsin until he was nine years old. His father wasn't around, but still he thought of those years as the happiest of his childhood. Men need strong male role models, and we seek them out when we don't have them. When Rick's mother remarried, he hoped his new stepfather would be that role model, but he very quickly found out that wouldn't be the case. He could do nothing but standby and watch, terrified, as his stepfather physically abused his mother regularly.

"It wasn't just a push or a smack when I saw it," Rick told me, "it was a full-blown punch on a woman."

When his mother had finally had enough, she and Rick packed as quickly as they could and drove to a battered women's shelter in California. Rick felt immediate relief to get away from the abuser in his life, and he was excited because his biological father also lived in California. He'd never met him, but we all long for that connection with our father, and on the day Rick met his dad he experienced pure joy.

He told Rick he'd be back in a week, but his dad didn't show up that next week. In fact, Rick hasn't seen his dad since.

Think about what that must have done to Rick's psyche and to his self-confidence. Think about how it must've made Rick's longing for a male connection even stronger.

A couple of years later, Rick found a male role model in his little league baseball coach, who was eager to play that part in Rick's life. Over the next few months, that coach became a trusted friend and mentor to Rick.

And then one day he violated that trust in a way that scared Rick, who didn't know how to react. He didn't know what to do when this man whom Rick had learned how to trust took advantage of him by sexually abusing him. Feeling scared and alone, Rick did nothing, and the abuse continued for years. That's a lot for anyone to endure, but I have to think it's especially hard for a 13-year-old boy who had never been given the chance to have a strong male role model in his life. Rick wasn't emotionally developed enough to see how he could move past the abuse his mentor was routinely subjecting him to, so he grabbed his belt and went to the closet with the intention of hanging himself.

With the leather belt strangling him, Rick's faith in God made him rethink his decision to commit suicide. He felt like his job on this planet hadn't been revealed to him yet and he needed to see it through. For years he endured the sexual abuse, which he told no one about. He also didn't tell anyone about his attempted suicide. Instead, he—like a lot of men—tried to "tough it out" and bury the pain deep inside himself while presenting the world with a strong jaw and a straight face.

The United States Air Force provided an escape for Rick. He enlisted as soon as he turned 18 years old and he had a successful military career without ever having to divulge to anyone the secret that he had been sexually abused and on the brink of suicide as a teenager. He didn't divulge it to his wife during their marriage that eventually failed. He didn't divulge it to the friends he'd meet for beers. He walked with that knowledge all by himself for 30 years, and didn't have any idea of what doing life would be like if he ever shared those secrets with someone else. Getting comfortable keeping secrets is a good way to not communicate with those you need to communicate with. Rick's second marriage was experiencing a communications breakdown and it was probably on its way to failing when his mother-in-law tagged him in the comments of a School of Man video on Facebook.

Rick said when he watched that video, he saw "a bunch of men exercising and doing some crazy stuff and it was totally not for me."

As I've said, the physical stuff doesn't always appeal to our guys, but then Rick saw some of the other videos, the stories of who some of the School of Man participants actually are and the transformations they had experienced because of the program. These were grown-ass men. Powerful, strong men, digging into their pasts, admitting their faults, and embracing their vulnerabilities in order to be better in the present and the future for those they love and for themselves. That's something Rick recognized he needed in his life. He wanted to be a better father and husband. So he signed up.

Rick lived in New Mexico at the time, so he did the work as part of our virtual boat crew, but he adhered to the curriculum at every turn. He participated in the exercises and the calls and he learned to trust the other men in Class 002 of School of Man. These guys rallied around each other and they rallied around Rick, who had never had any long-term male role models who didn't treat him like something easily disposed of. Think of what that means for a man to suddenly be a part of a brotherhood he never thought was possible.

This is why we do what we do at School of Man. Not that everyone who comes through our program has a story like Rick's, but most of us have some kind of demon in our past or in our present that we can face if we just have the right encouragement from other men. Rick's story is one of my favorites because I can see what a difference it made in his life to be unburdened by the pain he felt. When he learned it's okay to be vulnerable, and when he learned to trust other men—his classmates—he told them his secrets and wouldn't you know they didn't act how he always thought people would if they knew his deep, dark secret. School of Man provides the right type of environment for men to reveal who they are because we support each other.

Having that type of environment changed Rick Pena's life. Talking to his School of Man brothers about the things he had kept hidden away for so long gave him the courage he needed to talk to his wife, Courtney. By revealing himself and his past to her, she could better understand where he came from, which helped her better comprehend who she was even married to. And on top of that, School of Man teaches our guys to hold each other accountable and take ownership of their own behavior. The result for Rick and his wife is that their communication breakdown began to correct itself.

Rick buried his shame because he thought no one would love him if he shared his past with them. But, of course, Courtney loved him even more because he was strong enough and he trusted her enough to reveal himself. From the outside looking in, that seems obvious, but when you're living it, you feel like you're living it all by yourself, so it can be a really hard lesson to learn.

PART THREE

LIFE, LOVE, AND LEGACY

14

THE WORK

The list of hardships that men face goes on and on—we all face some kind of hardship in our past—but that doesn't mean we have to let it dictate our future, or even our present. School of Man is about teaching men to get control of the life they have and deal with their hardships in a healthy way. To face those hardships rather than running away from them.

After someone's experience in School of Man is all over, after a class member satisfies all the requirements of School of Man, after he actively participates in 16 weeks of a physically, emotionally, and mentally rigorous curriculum and successfully endures the Crucible, he earns his Phoenix. But the work doesn't stop there. In a way, it's just the beginning. None of us are perfect, I can promise you that. We aren't offering guys a finishing school as much as we're offering to equip them with an arsenal of weapons and tools they can use to navigate their lives with both strength and humility.

It takes more work for some than it does others, but there's nothing wrong with that. The only thing that matters is that you are willing to accept that work needs to be done and you have the courage to stare it down. You can be "successful" without being fulfilled. There is a major difference between achievement and fulfillment. There are plenty of guys out there who are chasing, chasing, chasing, and a lot of the time they're catching what they think they want, but then they're confused when they aren't fulfilled, so they target something else that will have the same result. That's why we've got multi-millionaires who have succeeded at nearly every turn and then one day commit suicide. A man like that can have all the money in the world and it won't make him happy enough to spare his own life. Or you can have a guy who's making minimum wage and barely squeaking by, but he loves what he's doing, and he loves his family and that's enough for him. The point is this: It's about more than money and other measurements of what society thinks of as success. It's about knowing your authentic self, being comfortable in that knowledge, and then building relationships based on it. It's about existing without your mask.

At School of Man, we are a brotherhood basking in that existence. The bonds our guys make with each other are the bonds that will last a lifetime. We've got a network of men spread across this country, from all different backgrounds, working in all kinds of different professions, fighting all kinds of different demons, in various states of physical, mental, and emotional shape, but every one of them can pick up the phone right now and know with confidence they can call more than a handful of men who will help them with the issues they're facing. They'll do it without casting judgment and without listening to them passively.

But it's not just about coping with what life throws at you. It's also about learning that you can't die with your dreams. You owe it to yourself and those you love to take the risk you're afraid of taking. But you also can't let an upper limit effect—the idea that you don't deserve the things that make you happy, or that you must stay in your "safe zone"—hamper you.

These are guys who have learned to cut through the bullshit and hold each other accountable. They won't tolerate excuses, but they will tolerate a man strong enough to be vulnerable. These guys are doing life together in a way that's more rewarding than most people experience, and they're doing it together. I know because I get to be a part of it, and I'm incredibly proud of it. And I'm proud of each and every one of them. And I'm proud of myself. That's what School of Man teaches every day.

15

THE PHOENIX

So, if the real work starts after graduation from the School of Man, we want to give our members as many resources as we can to help them succeed in that work. In addition to our active public social media presence, we also have private Facebook groups for alumni of the program. The guys post things there in the group that they find inspiring and motivational, and they stay connected with each other, which provides the accountability they've grown accustomed to. But of course, they connect as individuals as well. Nothing makes me happier than to see one of them post something to their own personal Facebook profiles, and then a flood of their School of Man brothers respond with words of encouragement. Social media—Facebook, Instagram, Twitter, Snapchat, Tik Tok, and God knows what the next big fresh hell will be—can be an extremely negative place that takes a detrimental effect on us an individuals, but the more we commit to prioritizing positive relationships that matter, the more grounded we'll be in the aspects of life that matter. I'm talking about real friendships that don't require masks. People have a tendency to let loose on social media because they're sitting at home, protected by the distance of the Internet. Having a strong accountability network you can trust built up that will engage you in your everyday interactions helps keep you grounded in reality and makes it easier to shake off the haters, as they say. Why should you feel torn down by some lazy asshole online who doesn't know you when you've got brothers you've sweat with reminding you of what you can accomplish? You shouldn't feel torn down at all.

I mentioned earlier that after our guys successfully complete the Crucible, they earn their Phoenix. A phoenix, of course, comes from ancient Greek mythology and is a bird that has the ability to experience a rebirth. It arises from the ashes of its predecessor to become something new, and theoretically, better. The symbolism of that matches up with the experience of what our men go through when they arise anew from the School of Man. The man who rises up out of the Crucible is a better man than the one who entered the class months before. We give each graduate a coin they can hang onto as a reminder of the work they've put in, what they've accomplished, and the brotherhood they can always rely on.

The coin shows a helmet tilted down, resting atop a vertical sword's handle, which represents the humble warrior. The business end of the sword is being dipped into flames—forged in the fire, if you will, just like a man who needs to be strengthened. Coming out of each side of the sword are large, feathered wings fanned out in two half-circles, filling up the bulk of the coin's circumference. That's where the phoenix comes into play.

The coin is essentially worthless if you were to find it on the street, but the currency it holds for the School of Man is priceless. Here's how Phillip Iverson (Class of 004) described its importance:

> I completed the Crucible so I could earn a coin, but not for the coin itself. This coin I carry is a physical reminder every time I touch it and see it of all the growth (physical, mental, emotional, spiritual) that I went through over that weekend in May. This coin reminds me that I can do hard things and push myself. When I make contact with that coin, I remember that I am so much more than I give myself credit for and can do so much more. I remember that I have a band of brothers with whom I have fought through thick and thin with to realize that brotherhood and unity are real and alive. I am reminded that my limits are only set by myself and that I am allowed to challenge them every day. I am born anew in that I know I can fight for those things that matter and need to do so when it matters and comes to my *Why*. I remember that I am a new man who is stronger and better today than before and only improving every day—by at least 1%. So the coin is important because of what it represents, but in and of itself it's only a coin. I am a Phoenix.

Mac, Phillip's classmate—and a lot of other guys for that matter—has carried his Phoenix coin in his pocket every single day since he got it. He doesn't leave the house without it. Occasionally he would pull it out to show people, but then he worried about scratching it up, so he got a little pouch he puts it in. Now he rarely pulls it out, but whenever he struggles or experiences self-doubt, he reaches into his left pocket and feels for that pouch with the coin in it. He puts it in the center of his palm or he twirls it between his fingers. It's his grounding device. A reminder to put things into perspective. He relies on that coin so much that he got the image of it tattooed on his chest. That way, if for whatever reason, he loses that coin, he's still got the reminder inked into his skin for the rest of his life.

So you can see how that coin—a simple artifact—strengthens that connection our guys have with an important time in their lives. It's a tangible item symbolizing an intangible feeling that can only exist in a real-world experience through unmatched physical effort and mental fortitude achieved through School of Man.

16

LEAD WITH IMPACT

The Phoenix coin is a passive resource, but we've also got some more active ones. I love podcasts, and I have probably listened to a thousand of them. I'm big fan of The Joe Rogan Experience, The Tim Ferriss Show, and Jocko Willinick's podcast on leadership and discipline. There are others I like, but those are probably my favorites and give you an example of where my tastes lie. I like hearing the stories they've got people on to tell, and I draw inspiration from those. Underneath all of those stories is this: We all have 86,400 seconds in a day, but we never know when that one-second contract—the one that will change it all—is going to expire. Some of the most powerful stories that I've ever listened to are from the men who have been through our program, their wives, as well as everyday people who are in my life. I feel this way, and I think if each of you take a second and look around at who you're surrounded by, you'll also realize we are all walking amongst giants. Despite that, how often do we actually listen to the stories people around us share, take them in, and make ourselves better from them? We started the School of Man Podcast podcast to challenge our School of Man participants to do just that.

The podcast is one of the few aspects of the program that's actually available to the public, though, so in a way I'm challenging even those not involved in the program to focus on two things:

1. The relationships you have in your life. That could be your family and those who love you the most, your team at work, people you mentor, or anyone else.

2. The impact that you make on those relationships.

One of my favorite quotes comes from Steve Jobs. He says, "We're here to put a dent in the universe. Otherwise, why else even be here?" The podcast is an outlet that showcases everyday people who live that ethos.

One of my favorite quotes comes from Steve Jobs. He says, "We're here to put a dent in the universe. Otherwise, why else even be here?" When I set out on the mission to found School of Man, my vision became crystal clear - be the most impactful organization for men on the planet. I don't care about being the largest. I don't care about having Facebook ads constantly filling up a man's feed telling him how great we are and that we can change his life in 72 hours. That's complete bullshit by the way. Instead, what I care about is that a man walks away feeling fulfilled, accomplished, but above all, loved and reborn.

And if there is one thing I have learned about myself, and other men like myself, we struggle with communication, in particular asking for help. It is down right hard. This is one of the traits of an unhealthy alpha. Honestly, I do not think that a man wakes up one day and says to himself, "Today is the day I am going to burn it all down." Instead, throughout the span of his life or even in a particular season of life, he makes small little decisions that add up over time. He walks into the house and drinks one whiskey, which eventually turns into three. He starts waking up later. He quits reading. He quits talking to his spouse and goes into his dark corner and begins to hide in plain sight. He wears a mask when he is talking to his buddies. He wears a mask when he makes a sales presentation. He wears a mask when he is talking to his wife. But when he goes to bed is when it really hits him hard. All the fear, anxiety, and insecurities flood his mind and like wrestling an alligator he tosses and turns with these thoughts until he finally says enough is enough before it is too late.

This is exactly where my brother, Doug was in the spring of 2021.

It was a normal spring day when I received a call from Doug. Leading up to this call, he had been somewhat a ghost. I think it is important to know, when entering into the School of Man, outside of showing up with a present mindset, proactive communication is at the top of the list when it comes to standards. Why? Because we as men are not very good at communicating like I had mentioned above. More importantly, we are not very good at communicating the important things to those we love the most. This is why a no call, no show is not only frowned upon in the organization, but it raises a red flag. So, when Doug, who is not only a legacy member but a leader within SoM, started avoiding calls and texts I knew something was wrong.

Immediately, myself along with my fellow brothers in SoM

went on the offensive. Finally, Doug started communicating with us and then the call finally came.

This type of call is a call I do not like to receive, but when the call comes through you need to understand you were chosen for a reason. When you answer it, you better be ready to lead with impact. I remember the call vividly because I was sitting in a chair, staring out the window in my bedroom. When I answered the phone, I knew something was wrong. I knew one of my brothers had gone to a dark place and he was doing the bravest thing anyone could and that is raise his hand.

When I answered, I said, "Doug, tell me where you are and let me know that you are okay."

I could see the tears rolling down his face through the phone. It took him a minute to collect himself and then he answered, "Cole, I am raising my hand. I need help. I have not slept a wink in over a week. I am simply a mess."

Being here before, I simply listened with intent. I did not say a word, instead I let him pour his heart out. When you have a man who is in pain, it is easy to go into fix it mode, because that is what we have been trained to do. The reality however is that he will not be able to download the information you are telling him, so you have to be strategic with your mentorship. This is where Doug was, but I knew when the moment presented itself, I had to snap him out of it which I knew Doug would respond to the tough love.

As he slowly came to a close that is when I took my shot and I immediately led with the right hook.

"Doug, now you listen to me. I am coming to see you. You can't tell me no. You can't tell me you don't need help. Everything that I say goes from this point moving forward. You got it?"

He was reluctant at first, but then finally caved. This man had not slept in a week. He found himself at the bottom of the bottle. And he went to the place where no man should ever be and that is contemplating taking his life.

Immediately after I hung up the phone I talked to Ashley about what was going on and she agreed that I needed to get on a plane at the first chance to be with Doug.

After booking the flight I personally felt this tug at my heart and my why once one more became crystal clear to me. God has put me on this earth to liberate men. This has nothing to do with me, but it has everything to do with impact. Off I went.

Landing in Atlanta, Doug was there to pick me up. I knew at first he was going to do his best to put on a front as if everything was okay, but it wasn't 24 hours prior that I sat on the phone for over an hour while he sobbed. Acting as if he was okay, I knew he was not. When he saw me, he gave me the biggest hug and cried on my shoulder. I held him as tight as I possibly could as a brother should and knew it was time to go to work. And that is what we did.

Over the course of the following days I gave Doug tough love, but helped him build a system to get him moving in the right direction. We woke early, meditated, journaled, exercised, and just hung out. It honestly was good for the both of us. Although this would not repair the hole in his heart, progress truly does equal happiness and when a man is tired, beaten, and tormented he is in his most vulnerable state to learn. That's where Doug was. All we were looking to do was light the spark so he could get back to being healthy.

So, what triggered all of this? Doug's marriage abruptly ended after 22 years. This triggered depression and anxiety. At the age of 60, Doug had felt as if he was a failure and that there was no hope for him in the future. Coupled with alcohol this is a dangerous place to be in. It is not a permanent place, but so many men imprison themselves and never ask for help. Doug did the bravest thing any man could do and that was raise his hand. He did not let pride get in the way, he trusted the process, and admitted that he was perfectly flawed.

As I write this, Doug is on fire right now. He is the hero his children need and the man that looks back in the mirror is the man he loves to see. In SoM, he is leading men through his story and he is younger than he has ever been. It is amazing how some of the most painful times in your life are the most beautiful. It takes courage to look at it that way, but when you do, you are ready to lead with impact.

This is Doug's story to tell, not mine. That's why I encourage you to listen to our podcast episode together. Here is a real man, with a real story, that executes real impact. I personally left a lot of details out for a variety of reasons, but when you listen to the episode you will get the full experience.

I will leave you with this. Impact is the single most important gift you can give to this world. It is the secret to life and what generates fulfillment which is what we all seek. It requires you to put your interest aside and serve others. It doesn't mean you have to jump on a plane and go help someone a few states over. You can first start with yourself, then start in your home. It is the small things that increase over time and I can promise you that you will be amazed how much you grow in the process.

17

IF NOT YOU, THEN WHO?

School of Man is a vehicle, a platform, the name we give to our community of men. Someone had to create it, to give it that name, to provide the physical and virtual space where we could all exist amongst each other. When things were kicking off and School of Man was merely a dream for me, I knew deep down I wanted to follow that dream, but floating around inside my head were all the reasons I could think that forming this brotherhood would be a bad idea. Why do we carry around all this negative self-talk when what we really need to ask is *If not me, then who?*

That's the mantra of an organization I love called the Travis Manion Foundation, headquartered in Pennsylvania, but they've got offices in major cities across the country. The foundation takes its name from U.S. Marine Corps 1st Lt. Travis Manion, who died in 2007 while on patrol with the 1st Reconnaissance Battalion in Iraq's Al Anbar province. His platoon was ambushed and Travis led a counterattack against enemy forces. He tried to draw enemy sniper fire away from his wounded teammates, and while it saved everyone else in his patrol, it cost Travis his life. Before his deployment to Iraq, Travis explained his sense of duty using that mantra: "If Not Me, Then Who?"

He felt called to serve his country and he wasn't afraid to answer that call. Talk about someone to use as a model, Travis Manion didn't die lying down on his back, or running from the life he wanted; he died living. An entire foundation sprung up around Travis's mindset and it's inspiring more and more people every day.

The Travis Manion Foundation's chief operating officer is a graduate of the School of Man, and his work is always a strong reminder to me to answer the call, whatever it may be. As a leader and mentor, I always challenge my guys to think about what it is in their life that would best be answered with Travis Manion's mantra.

I had one of my guys come to me and say he wants to start his own business, but he's scared of the financial risks involved in such a thing. My response to him was "If not you, then who?" And what I'm really saying is *You are enough. You are capable of conquering whatever's in front of you. No matter what the situation is and no matter what circumstances you're under.* Answer that question—If not me, then who?—and then raise your hand and say, "I am ready. Come on, give it to me. Give me the pressure. Put my back up against the wall, so that way I can just move forward."

If not me, then who? That's something we should ask ourselves not just when we're thinking about taking a step forward in a business venture or making a significant change to our place in the world, it's something we should ask ourselves all the time. For me, *If not me, then who* for Ashley? *If not me, then who* for my kids, Landon and Ava Madison? Asking myself that question is a reminder that I was called to do something bigger than live a life in which I wake up, work, eat, sleep, and die. I was called to live, to impact others on a grander scale, to mentor, to coach, to awaken the dead when it comes to certain aspects of men's lives—to help center them and make sure that their family is good. I was called to help men reestablish themselves within their homes. I was called to help men in my situation who are called to do something bigger, but who are also refusing to lean in. I was called to help them have enough faith in themselves and their abilities so that they can actually take the leap they want to take. Because what they create may help put food not only on their family's table, but on other people's tables, and serve their fellow man at a high level. I see that, I feel that, I believe that.

We can all stand to ask ourselves, If not me, then who? How can you apply it to your life? And more importantly, what does your answer call you to do? It's important to be honest in your response to yourself. It's your job as well as mine to put a dent in the universe—no matter what the media says, no matter what the message trending on social media is—so focus right now on what you can and should do to put a dent in the universe. Lead with impact.

18

WHAT WE DO IN THE DARK

To make that dent, every man and woman needs to erase a certain statement from our minds. It's not a long statement, and hopefully it's not one any of us uses every day, but it's one we've all probably told ourselves and maybe others at least once in our lives.

No one will ever know.

What we do in the dark will show itself in the light. That's a statement I tell my guys all the time because it carries a training aspect with it that I love. Here's what it means to me: Imagine a prizefighting boxer who's on top of the world, every major sports news network has their cameras pointed at him while he talks a big game, but then he goes six months without doing any training, and so when he finally climbs back into the ring, he gets his ass kicked in the bright lights on pay-per-view. It's clear to everyone who watches the fight that he didn't put in the work when he should have, when the cameras weren't rolling.

No one will ever know is the malicious statement that undermines the very idea behind the statement *What we do in the dark will show itself in the light.*

We all have our own examples of when this statement crops up, but let me tell you when I see it in my own life and in the lives of guys I talk with. The low-hanging fruit here is when it shows up in the gym.

I love physical training and working with guys to help make themselves into warrior athletes. Seeing people set, meet, and exceed their fitness goals gives me as much satisfaction as when I exceed my own goals—that's one of the main reasons I started School of Man. From my early days of mentoring, I have always been willing to give my time, energy, and resources to help someone else, but I need them to commit to giving as much to themselves. That's why I needed a commitment from Adam when we first started training together. And that's why we ran Zack through that brutal workout when he wanted to join us. Nothing makes me turn my head and question a man's character more than anything as when a guy cuts reps in the gym. If a man cuts reps in the gym, and another man partnering with the first man allows him to cut reps, those two guys lack integrity in my book. Let me tell you why that bothers me so much.

If a workout calls for 12 rounds, let's say the guy does eight of them. And then someone calls him out for it.

"Hey, what's up? Why aren't you putting in all the reps?"

The guy will defend himself with one of a thousand excuses, but every one of them are bullshit. This is how the prizefighter ends up getting his ass kicked when the lights are shining on him, because he didn't put in the work. Even worse, let's say he's not a boxer, but a football player—now he's cheating not just himself, but he's also cheating his team because they were depending on him to put in the work so they could all succeed. But that's just how it translates in sports.

Let's talk about how *No one will ever know* translates in a marriage, and I'll reference my own as an example. White lying damn-near crushed my marriage. The ability to tell a white lie is the little voice inside your head that says, "No one will ever know." When my wife would call, for instance, here's the form that mindset could take.

"Hey, babe. Are you coming home?" Ashley would ask when I was at a happy hour for work.

"Yeah, I'm on my way," I would say. But really, I was still drinking.

When I showed up at home an hour later, when I should've been home 45 minutes earlier, a fight erupts all because I told myself when she called that no one would ever know if I stayed at the bar a few more minutes. It seemed innocent enough and I didn't think Ashley would have me on the clock, but why shouldn't she? She asked me a direct question, and I gave her a direct answer. My white lie eroded the truth, and also my credibility in my wife's eyes. In the same way a man cheating reps can no longer be trusted to put in the work. Nobody wants to workout with someone who's shortcutting their way through a workout, much less be married to them. Same concept, bigger stakes.

Here's another one I see and hear about from guys. Married men who flirt with a server or another random woman when they're out with their coworkers or friends—and it's a two-way street; married women do this same thing. *No one will ever know.*

I could go on and on with examples of where this statement shows up in the lives of the men I work with. There are the guys who made a habit out of popping those prescription pills because they thought no one would ever know. The guys who develop an addiction to porn because they think no one will ever know. The guys who have put down the bottle, but then took a sip because no one will ever know. And the next thing he knows, he can't put it down again, and he has to keep telling a lie bigger than the last one to try to convince his family the mask he's wearing is actually not a mask and they look like a fool because it's obviously a mask. All because of that one little white lie. That one little statement. *No one will ever know.*

The list is endless, and I've seen more men be toppled after having made it to the top of their respective mountain because of it. It doesn't matter how much work they put in to get there, it can all be undone when they refuse to eradicate *No one will ever know* from their lives. And, trust me, it is a freaking climb back up that mountain after you've rolled down it.

It sounds easy when it's all in black and white, but I know it's hard, which is why I don't mean to sound like I'm sitting in a place of judgment. I have screwed up, I have tripped over my own feet, and I have failed more than I can even account for because of that utterly self-destructive mindset.

You have to want to build a reputation for yourself that you are proud of. Have integrity in every aspect of your life. Be in control of where your life is taking you. That's a tall drink of water, but I'd rather drink from that than cut corners because when you cut corners you start telling those little white lies and adopting that mindset that *No one will ever know.* That's the kind of thinking that will snowball on you until you are no longer in control of your life. You will no longer know who you are.

All of us—men and women both—are going to screw up. We're human. It's as plain and simple as that. But we have to recognize that and take ownership of it. Tell the truth because what you do in the dark will eventually show itself in the light. Audit that in your life. No one is perfect, but you can always pivot and stop the drift. Turn that limiting belief into an atomic, liberating truth. Build the reputation you want. The one that will take your life in the direction you want. Don't cheat the rep, no matter what "the rep" looks like in your life. Work hard. Earn your way. Don't be entitled. Be honorable. Be courageous. Be a leader.

19

GRATITUDE

When you take on the role of being a leader—in any aspect of your life—that brings with it a lot of responsibility, and with responsibility comes more decisions, some of which will be hard. It's easy to make mistakes, but again, take ownership of those mistakes and you can get through your failures and prepare for the next difficult decision you've got to make. I've found that one of the most important things you can do to get over your failures is to maintain a heart full of gratitude.

I have ways I do that. First, let me say, my family always taught me to be grateful for what we had, so I'll admit that gives me a head start, but no matter what your upbringing looked like, it's never too late to practice a few methods that will keep you grateful for the opportunities you face every day.

Every time the Earth completes a rotation, the sun rises on a new day for each of us. I wake up early and on days when I get to start my morning with a workout at School of Man Headquarters in Little Rock, I try to take in the sunrise with the guys. It's one of the prettiest places to watch the sun come up in the city—and I'd say that even if I weren't surrounded with my brotherhood, but of course, having them there definitely adds to the experience. Regardless of where I am, though, the sun coming up in the morning reminds me that I have a new lease on life. No matter what happened the day before, I get another chance to be the man I want to be, and I need to make the most of it.

We are always on a field of diamonds, whether we realize it or not. As a man, we must treat every day as if it's our last. I know that's a sobering thought, but it's an important one because it helps us focus on what matters most. That's why it's in the first paragraph of the School of Man ethos.

Think about your own heart. Think honestly of the struggles people in the world are going through right now. Maybe you're actually struggling yourself, but remember this: We all have a choice. That's the single greatest life force that we all have. You can choose how you approach your day. It's as plain and simple as that, so try approaching it with gratitude first. Fill your heart with gratitude.

On days when I take the time to look and be thankful for what I have, I'm giving myself a much better position from which to start my day. When I compare my struggles with the plight of others, it's hard not to be grateful. And I'm not even talking about people in third-world countries. I'm talking about people I know. Ashley has a friend whose child passed away recently. That's tough. Obviously that's the kind of thing that will grip you hard. I can't even imagine what I would do if something happened to my kids. That would overshadow everything on my plate right now that I might think is a struggle. And so how can I not be grateful?

Regardless of your circumstances, the one thing you can always choose to be as a man is to be grateful. You can even be grateful for the hard times. I know that sounds silly, weird, or counter-intuitive, but it's true. I've found a lot of strength when I've had to endure adversity, and I always found myself to be a better man when I eventually came out okay on the other side of that adversity.

When I'm facing something that pulls me down, I take a second to recount the things I should be grateful for. Just as important as naming those things, I need to detail *why* I'm grateful for each of them. That's how I remind myself that I'm living in a field of diamonds. A lot of people will say, "Yeah, Cole, I know what I'm grateful for, and I know why I'm grateful for those things," but it's not enough to simply think about them and keep a list in your head. Write them down. Keep a physical list.

I use what I call my Jar of Awesome. I got it from Tim Ferriss and it works really well. The idea is that when something happens during the week that fills me with gratitude, I'll pull out a pen and little piece of paper. I'll write it down and put that piece of paper in the Jar of Awesome. They don't even have to be big things—sometimes I write down that I'm thankful for having a hot shower or a hot meal or getting a good night's rest. Other times, I'll write down that I closed a deal at work that I'm thankful to have the relationships I do with those that I love and those willing to square me up to make me better. At any given moment, I know I have those things, but it's the act of sitting down to reflect on it that makes me feel truly fulfilled in my life.

When I write those things down and put them in the Jar of Awesome, I can always see those pieces of paper in the jar. Ava Madison and Landon do it with me, which is a good practice for them, and it helps remind me of the good things that have happened for my family, as well.

"I'm grateful I can do the splits on my back," my daughter wrote one day.

Another day she wrote, "I love hope."

I don't know what inspired her to write that, but I like knowing that something did. That's why I encourage you to get your family involved in marking the things in your life they should be grateful for. As a man, your ultimate responsibility is to grow your family.

We're better people when we pay attention to every good, bad, and ugly we have in our lives, but sometimes when we are facing the bad and the ugly, it's a life-saver to be able to pull out a slip of paper from the Jar of Awesome. Even remembering the smallest things you're grateful for can help you keep the bad things in perspective. Before you know it, you can literally see that your jar will be full.

It's not about the money grabs or the medals I earned as much as it is about finding fulfillment and putting a dent in the universe. Everyone can do that. We're all created to be unique and no matter where we are or how we got to that point, we all carry with us that single greatest power force of choice. It's up to you to use it for the betterment of yourself, your family, and those around you.

Seek out gratitude. Speak out gratitude. Who gives a shit what anyone else is doing? Who gives a shit that you've got a hundred emails in your inbox, or that you've got to return a dozen phone calls? Just take a few minutes in your day to truly be grateful for the things that you have, rather than thinking about the things that you don't have. I promise you if you make a habit out of doing that, you'll become a more fulfilled man. That's what it's all about.

The world will reciprocate the gratitude that you put into it. In 2014, Matthew McConaughey won the Oscar for Best Actor for his fantastic performance of Ron Woodroof in Dallas Buyers Club. He gave what I think is one of the best acceptance speeches of all time. In that speech, he said he needs three things each day:

1. Something to look up to.
2. Something to look forward to.
3. Someone to chase.

He looks up to God because God "graced [his] life with opportunities" and has shown him that "it's a scientific fact that gratitude reciprocates." He looks forward to his family because his dad taught him how to be a man—as a dad should a son—and his mother taught him to respect himself and therefore respect others, and he wants to make his wife and kids proud. His hero to chase? Himself in 10 years. When he turned 15 years old, his hero was himself at 25. And at 25, himself at 35.

"You see, every day, and every week, and every month, and every year of my life, my hero is always ten years away," he said. "I'm never going to be my hero. I'm not going to obtain that and that's fine with me because it keeps me with somebody to keep on chasing."

Just like McConaughey, we've got to keep on chasing the best version of ourselves, and making time to fill our hearts with gratitude puts us in a position to best accomplish that. I'm as highly charged as they come—I am always in pursuit of success, always on to the next thing, always ready to conquer the task ahead of me—but to really find fulfillment, I've got to slow down and appreciate the things around me. Fulfillment lies in the things I have more than in the things I don't have, and all I have to do to remember that, is to have a look around.

Watching my kids set and achieve a goal fills my cup all the way up. We live on a kind of hill, and I watched Landon ride his bike up the hill to the neighbor's mailbox. Then he tried again and he made it to the mailbox two doors down. And then three doors down. And so on and so forth until he made it up the hill and around the block. It's not far, but to him, it's a huge accomplishment. Seeing him do that is the stuff that really brings me joy and makes me happy. More than that, it restores a sense of adventure in me that I had as a boy, but forgot about at some point in my adult life. That happens to all of us, I think, but we can gain it back if we're open to it.

A lot of men go to great lengths to attempt to recreate that sense of adventure they had as a kid. But I promise you that it doesn't take an elaborate trip. You don't have to go backpacking through the mountains or shoot an elk. If that's something you want to do, good for you—rock and roll—but maybe the adventure you're looking for is right in front of your face, with your kid. Maybe it's just playing with them. They still have that wonder about them that you're willing to chase to other continents. Engage with them. Help them build that tent or that fort at the house. Join them in that imaginative state of mind. I tell all you dads out there to man up and be a kid again. Quit searching for the fountain of youth through life hacks. Instead, laugh, play, and have fun with those who love you the most. Own the damned day.

My wife will gladly tell you that I'm the biggest kid in the Rodgers household. I love a good Nerf war. I love to bag bad guys. I absolutely love it.

Not too long ago, I talked with one of my guys in the School of Man who felt like he lacked adventure in his life. He wanted to take a trip that would test him physically and show him a new part of himself, but this was during the COVID-19 pandemic, which limited travel, of course. All he could think about was what the pandemic kept him from doing and frustrated him more than anything. I helped him reframe the way he was approaching the problem.

"Don't tell me what you can't do," I said. "Tell me what you can do."

By reshaping the situation like that I essentially asked how he can make the best out of the current circumstances. There are men who have spent time as prisoners of war who still found ways to make the best out of their circumstances because they distracted themselves with the things they could control so they wouldn't be forced into the line of thought that they had been stripped of everything.

Humans are innately greedy beings and we want to lay claim to everything we see. Even as children, one of the first concepts they understand is "Mine!" They think every toy they pick up belongs to them. Every piece of food on the table is theirs. As parents, we have to teach our kids to share, which is a concept that's generally accepted across the board—at least for our kids. But in our lives, we're out there saying, "Mine!" to pretty much everything we can get our hands on. We only share things when it comes to someone we really trust and care for.

What's more is that we see the things other people have laid claim to and think we should have those things, too. That's a problem infinitely compounded with the advent of social media. There are more than 1 billion people on Facebook and most of them are constantly showcasing the best versions of their lives. They are taking vacations, buying expensive homes, clothes, cars, meals. It's natural to think we also deserve to take those vacations and buy those things. We want to keep up with the Joneses, so we obsessively focus on the things we don't have, rather than enjoying the things we do have.

It's the same concept for the guy who called me thinking his life lacked adventure because his own quarantine during the pandemic had trapped his mind. And adventure doesn't have to be something as grand as whitewater rafting down the Colorado River or minimalist backpacking through the Alaskan wilderness. Yes, those are great trips, but we can't always take those. Think about a man trapped as a prisoner of war for years and what an adventure might look like to him? What would he give for a day spent playing Cops and Robbers with his son? Or taking his daughter down to the creek in the neighborhood to skip rocks across the water for a few hours? Life itself is an adventure if we're willing to see it as such. Our kids are more than ready to take that mindset and they'll always be thankful you do the same.

Stop thinking about the deadlines you're facing and the bills you have to pay and your never-ending to-do list, and find that playful inner child for a while. That's where your adventure lies, no matter what your circumstances. Be grateful for what you have and love those who love you the most.

20

MAINTAIN PERSPECTIVE

Nothing has really put that into perspective over the last few years—and probably longer than that—than the COVID-19 pandemic. That guy who called seeking adventure was not the only person feeling that. It all happened so fast, that there was no planning for it. Events got cancelled, one after the other until it seemed like our entire calendars were wiped out. All the plans we'd made to do things together suddenly vanished and we were left much more isolated than most of us had ever been before. Most people's natural impulse is to focus on all the things that were no longer happening.

For example, in the fall of 2019, we had several men from the School of Man sign up for an Ironman 70.3 Triathlon, which consist of a 1.2-mile swim, 56 mile bicycle ride, and a 13.1 mile run, raced in that order. That's a big-time race that can kick an athlete's ass, so those of us who were going to do it started training. None of us were triathletes. None of us had much confidence in our swimming abilities and some of us were downright scared to get in the water. But that's part of the reason why we signed up—to conquer our fears and overcome the things that scare the hell out of us.

We signed up for the Ironman in Galveston, Texas. We chose that one for a few different reasons, but a big one is that it's considered a good beginner's course. The water temperature was supposed to be in the 70s, the course is flat and there would be wind coming off the ocean. We held each other accountable and kept training, kept swimming and biking and running every week to prepare, but then the COVID-19 panic hit and Ironman cancelled the event. People weren't happy about it, but they understood that a global health emergency is nothing to mess with, so they stopped training, I think.

Our group didn't stop, though. There were four of us who had committed to the race and we got together after the event had been cancelled and recommitted to completing an Ironman, regardless of whether our physical exertion would be done under the official Ironman brand or not. We didn't need the Ironman branding to prove to ourselves we could chase our lion.

Zack Cox coined the term IronSoM to stand for Iron School of Man and we kept to the grind. But why would we feel compelled to keep going when everyone else quit? I think our group always knew we would keep going. I don't think we ever really considered giving up.

"When the email came," Jon Kennon (Class 001) said about the cancellation notification we got from Ironman, "All it did was change the destination for me. I knew we couldn't go to Galveston, but we just had to figure out a way to do it somewhere by ourselves."

"I didn't sign up for Ironman to get a trophy or a t-shirt or a medal," Zack said. "I do these things to take myself to the next level and to break through the limitations I have for myself."

For me, I knew we had set goals and we'd created a lot of momentum to accomplish those goals, so it was most important to me to keep the momentum going, no matter where we ended up running the race. To maintain our momentum, we had to get creative and resourceful. Aristotle said, "It is during our darkest moments that we must focus to see the light," and we had to pull together with each other to focus to find a new location where we could create our own course.

I never even thought to get pissed off about the event not happening because I knew the guys I'd embarked on the Ironman journey with are the kind of guys who will figure things out and see it through. Hosting and competing in our own Ironman became a whole new kind of challenge that took on a life of its own. To be honest, it probably made the race way more special than it ever would have been had we gone to Galveston. It became much more about fulfillment than achievement at that point.

In the beginning, we planned to do the swim portion of the race in the lap pool at a local aquatic center in Little Rock, but then we had to adjust fire again when the center closed for the pandemic as well. Then we remembered that every year there's a triathlon in a small city about an hour south of Little Rock and they use DeGray Lake for the swim portion of the event.

I'd never been there before, so a week before the race, we went down to the lake where a friend let us stay at his lake house. We found a good spot to swim laps back and forth and gave it a good practice run, which allowed us to get acclimated to water colder than we were expecting. But there was no acclimating to the idea of swimming into open water for 1,000 meters and then turning around and swimming back. Especially for guys who don't feel comfortable in the water, but that's where our training comes into play. Zack summed it up well afterward.

"In those moments of discomfort when you're scared to death of what you're getting into, you really just have to fall back on your training. We trained hard for the event, and I knew we could do it, no matter what the course looked like. One foot at a time."

We all put in the work, and we all *knew* we'd put in the work. Even so, there's always going to be things that pop up on the fly you can't predict. Zack's heart started racing when we were in the water and he was full of anxiety. That happened a couple of times, but again, his training had taught him to pause, focus on where he was, and eventually his heart rate came back down, which relieved his anxiety and prepared him to finish the swim. You can ask Zack about the truth in this, but when you're testing your physical self like that and you start to lose it, that's where the meditation we do—the mental training—becomes crucial. That's one of the reasons we work with our guys on a holistic approach. And it gets them through more times than not.

For me, the swim didn't intimidate me nearly as much as the hills I'd seen when I went to scout the course. In Arkansas, lakes are surrounded by hills and the best place to do the course included these long ascents. I couldn't shake it out of my head that we were going to have to do this stretch twice to get the distance we needed to get. By the time we reached the cycling portion of our self-directed Ironman, I knew we were about to face a tough section of the race. We'd been training for a flat course in South Texas, but we ended up in hills in Central Arkansas. The relative difference felt like we were climbing Mount Everest. And on top of that, I couldn't help but feel like something was wrong with my bike. We'd done some training at a place called CliqueCycle and the instructor, Peter, could apply resistance to our bikes. Out there on the road, it felt like I was at CliqueCycle and Peter had turned my resistance all the way up, so that the effort I put in didn't accurately reflect the output the bike gave me.

In School of Man, when someone's making excuses, we say that person's inner bitch is coming out. It takes a lot to get my inner bitch to come out, but it was out that day. I knew something was wrong with my bike, but I didn't know how to fix it. We were on our second hill when I finally pulled over to take a look at it.

One of the guys said, "Man, there's something up with your bike. Maybe your gears aren't working or something."

"Nah," I said. "I'll get it. I'll find my groove soon."

But I didn't find that groove on the way out. Meanwhile, the other guys were crushing it.

"She giveth and she taketh away," Kennon kept saying, like a mantra, because we'd get to the bottom of a hill and get to relax for just a moment before having to go up another one.

We eventually made it to the 14 miles, to the first turn-around point and my inner bitch was in my head and questioning whether or not I'd be able to make it the whole way. We were looking at a 56-mile grind of rolling hills. I knew I'd already ridden more than 40 miles earlier in the week, so I thought I might be spent. Coming to that realization pissed me off. I was pissed at myself more than anything else because I couldn't figure out how to find my groove, and that got me to one of the lowest points I'd experienced in years.

I started cramping in my lats, my hamstrings, and my triceps, to the point that I started making a plan to modify my race. The hills were killing me. I thought about finishing by riding laps in the parking lot. I thought about forgoing the race as a participant to instead crew the other guys so they could finish. I was in a dark place.

To get through it, I had to tap into the gratitude I have for the things in my life. All of those things I knew that were written down on little slips of paper in my Jar of Awesome. All of the things I hadn't written down yet, but I knew were coming. A big one at that time for me was the fact that I knew my mom's last chemotherapy treatment was a week away. Keeping things like that in my mind where I can tap into it quickly motivates me. It lifted me out of that dark place during the race.

Another motivator that kept me going was that I was out there with guys from the School of Man, guys I care about and trust and who care about me and trust me. Later, I realized my back bicycle wheel was loose, which caused me some problems and made my bike less efficient. But I'm glad I endured. I'm glad it happened the way it did. It taught me some humility and reminded me that no matter how much I train, and no matter how on top of my game I feel, I always have more to learn.

The race humbled us all. Zack had his issue in the water with his heartrate. He questioned then if he had any business being in the water in the first place—should he be trying to complete an Ironman? Of course he should be. He'd put in the hours and done the work. Kennon did really well on the bike for 42 miles.

"I felt like a kid on bike until the last 14 miles," he said. He had an endless supply of energy and wanted to push through every chance he got.

But then something got in his head and his body started pulling all his energy into his core. From out of nowhere, just before a 1.8-mile climb, he had to fight a desire to give up. It devastated him mentally and made for a rough end to the bicycle section of the race. He really went to his dark side when he got off the bike and started in on the half-marathon run.

His legs were convulsing and in shock. He tried to walk it out. He hydrated and got a bite to eat, but he didn't feel like himself. He sent his wife a text message and told her about his struggle. Like any supportive partner, she reminded him of how prepared he was for this. That didn't make it any less hard for him—it kicked his ass—but he finished it.

Being with those guys for this race that we created for ourselves and overcoming the obstacles we faced while doing so turned out to be one of the most inspiring things I've been a part of. We all had pain. When Kennon came off that bike, I saw him grimace in pain. He's a tough guy with a warrior's heart, so when I saw that pain on his face, I knew he was hurting.

But we were all in it together and we kept moving as a single unit, determined to complete the task we'd set for ourselves. We stayed together and encouraged each other to keep going. Through the School of Man we have logged an endless number of miles, an endless number of hours in the gym, an endless number of phone calls and texts back and forth to deal with issues we've faced in our lives. We have proven to each other that we have each other's backs no matter how hard it gets. When we were in the hardest moments of that Ironman, there is no one we would have rather seen than each other. And that's how we were able to overcome every hardship and every weakness, all the way to the finish line.

Each man in the race had his specific obstacles to overcome, and each man also grew in his specific way, but we grew alongside each other. We all had to find an excuse to win in the moment. It was beautiful. And it started weeks before when Ironman cancelled the official race because of the global health crisis. Something that should have disappointed us, if we would have allowed it to. We never used that as an excuse to quit. Instead, we kept moving forward. We made it better. We found a greater fulfillment than we would have otherwise.

As a man, don't let your excuses get in the way for what you truly want to achieve in life. When you're hit with failure or adversity in life, don't back down. And know who will be right there beside you when the gunfire starts. If you don't have that community of men in your life, find it. Obviously, I think School of Man is a good place to do that, but it doesn't have to be with us. Take it upon yourself to find it somewhere. It's important to have men you can count on.

"I think y'all would have buddy-carried me on your backs if I wouldn't have been able to keep going," Kennon told us after we finished the race.

And do you know what we said?

"You're damn right we would have."

21

THE BUSINESS MODEL

Sometimes when I hear myself talk about the level of camaraderie and trust we have at the School of Man, it sounds
a bit like a utopian fraternity (and it can be), but I've got a
enough experience in the sales industry to pick up on the fact
when someone is probably trying to sell me something here.
So let me tell you why School of Man is different, and why we
have what is probably one of the worst business models out
there, and also why we have no plans to change it any time soon.
Anyone with any business sense would probably take a look at
it and say, "What the hell are you guys doing? This won't work."

I recently had a long phone conversation with a guy who's
interested in signing up. He would be in the virtual boat crew.
I asked him a lot of hard-hitting questions, we talked about his
life, and his goals.

"Well, where do I sign up?" he asked at the end of the
conversation.

"Man, I'll be totally candid with you," I said. "You sound like you have a ton of stuff going on in your life and I just don't know if you're going to be a good fit for the organization."

He paused, confused.

I explained that the School of Man is an organization that adheres to some fundamental principles, the first of which is *Impact*. We are the most impactful organization in the world for men—I guarantee it. There are a lot of organizations out there impacting men, so how can I say that we're the most impactful? Because of the relationships that form behind the scenes, in the day in and day out of self-discovery and trust-building. Those things happen very intentionally—they are not a byproduct of everything else that's happening within the curriculum. Those things *are* the curriculum. That's the only way to generate the results that our guys are seeking. We push them, we break them, we rebuild them. More accurately, they are going to push themselves, they are going to break themselves, they are going to rebuild themselves. The men in our organization are ultimately doing all the work that needs to be done.

Believe me when I say it's not a cake walk. Every man wants to be a part of the School of Man on a sunny day until we put him through the shit and make him deal with the mess, and that's what I told the guy on the phone.

"I respect that," he said. "I respect that you're willing to tell me I might not be a good fit for the School of Man because I figured you'd just want my money."

"Look at it this way," I said. "Every person has energy vampires in their lives and a lot of us buy the apps for our phones, we go to the two-day seminars, we buy the books, we hire a business coach or maybe a life coach, who probably knows nothing about life, and then all of the sudden, we're back at square one. We continue to do this hamster-wheel approach and expect a different result, which is of course...insanity. If I take everyone who is willing to pay the tuition, I'll be spending the majority of my time dealing with energy vampires rather than spending it with the men who are putting a dent in the universe. And I don't want that. That's why our recruitment process actively includes turning candidates down."

He couldn't believe it. He thought we were like everyone else and after his money above all else. Money is not the issue with School of Man. I have another job. Money has never been the issue. It's about impact for me. Yes, it takes money to operate School of Man, but the revenue will follow the impact that SoM has on this world.

A businessman who takes a glimpse at our business model will tell us our organization should fail out of the gate and not grow at all, much less thrive for a long period of time. But that's exactly what we're going to do because we're weeding out guys who only want to throw money at the problem. We're committed to only recruiting and retaining the best of the best. Plain and simple.

An undisciplined approach to growth is a dangerous, dangerous game, and speculating that any random man off the street is going to miraculously be a game-changer to his home and his community at any given time is complete and utter bullshit. Guys think they can coast on all their accomplishments and the reputation they've built. But regardless of their resume and their reputation, how are we supposed to know they aren't simply putting on a mask for us (and themselves)?

The resume the School of Man is interested in is built through consistent performance under pressure. We don't let someone into our coveted brotherhood until they have proven they are willing to put in the work. It's the same for the men who are joining up now as it was for Zack when Adam and I put him on the rower and asked him to prove himself. We want to see heart. Not everybody has it. Some people have heart all the time. Some people have it, but only when the time is right. We're looking for guys who have it and are ready to put it to work. Those are the guys who are a good fit for us.

In order for us to survive one hundred years or more, to be profitable—not just from an income perspective, but also from an energy and impact perspective—it requires the right people. We have to find the right people and put them on the right path to success in order for us to also be successful as an organization. Honestly, that means we have to say *no* more than we say *yes*. That's how we protect what makes the SoM special and continue to offer it to the men who are ready for it.

22

YOUR INNER WEIRDO

We aren't looking for guys who want to join a pack simply because it's a pack. We don't want guys who want to go with the flow. Only dead fish go with the flow. I want people who are ready to embrace their inner weirdo.

There are a lot of blog posts and books out there that talk about the common character traits of highly successful people. Some of them have some really well thought out hypotheses—successful people wake up early, have a routine, take risks, they're optimistic, outgoing, etc.—but I don't think it's that complicated. I know my own hypothesis is not especially scientific, but I think it all boils down to a person being willing to embrace their weirdness.

Every person in the history of the world that has been truly successful—famous people as well as people you know—have really put themselves out there and said "This is me, for better or worse." Take Elon Musk, for example. There's a guy worth nearly $90 billion (and counting) who refuses to be normal. He does not do things by the book. Instead he came out and made the bold statement that we're going to Mars. That's basically him throwing two middle fingers up into the air toward what's expected and saying, "We're going to go do this." It's the same thing with Steve Jobs, who held his middle fingers up to the computing standard of the time. Every successful person of any consequence held his or her middle fingers up to normality at a crucial point in their lives.

They know that if they don't step out to embrace the uncommon then nothing's going to happen. Instead, everybody's going to be stuck in a leadership vacuum. That's why they're such good models for what that character trait can really accomplish. In the School of Man, I preach that we're all weirdos if we'll let ourselves be. Look at me with my beautiful wife, beautiful children, I have a good job, and a nice house, so why would I subject myself to participating in the Crucible over and over? Because it reminds me of why I want to be uncommon. Because I wasn't created for common. If we were all the same, life would be boring.

It takes a certain level of weirdness to put yourself through School of Man. I assure you normal people do not subject themselves to 55 hours of unbelievably strenuous physical activity with little or no sleep. There's always a point in the Crucible where "normal" people who have no idea what we're doing will stop to watch us like we're animals in a zoo. They look at us like we're psychopaths because a normal way to exercise is to go into the gym and get on the elliptical or the treadmill, but instead, we're carrying a log around a public parking lot together or taking a mud bath. We're embracing that weirdo mindset because it reminds us that pain can be a thing of beauty for those who volunteer themselves to say, "You know what? I don't care what the world thinks of me. I'm going to step into my own. WE'RE GOING TO MARS, BABY!"

If you don't embrace that mindset, you'll never get what you want. As the saying goes: If I always do what I've always done, I'll always get what I've always got.

There are so many of us out there who get caught up in a cycle once we get out of school or the military. We graduate with student loan debt and we have to figure out a way to pay for that, so we get a job. And then we get married and then we take out a mortgage to buy a house and now we're in debt to that, too. Next thing you know, you look up and you're 20 years down the road and wondering how you're going to measure your life when you reach the end of it. We wonder what our legacy will be once we're gone.

For a long time, guys measured themselves by the title they carried within the organizations where they worked. And so when they had great ideas that didn't align with their identity within that organization, they didn't act on it. A lot of them weren't necessarily afraid of failure as much as they were afraid of what success might look like, and beyond that, they were afraid of how they would be viewed by their peers—family, friends, coworkers, or anyone else they see in their daily lives. They want to remain who they are because it's comfortable.

But nobody changes the world when they're comfortable. Normal people don't change the world. Zombies who are droning on through life don't change the world. You've got to make yourself uncomfortable to drive yourself to make the change in your own life and when you make the change in your own life, then maybe you can change the world. You've got to be willing to be weird in whatever that looks like in your life. In mine, it means carrying a log with my guys sometimes.

How do you challenge yourself to embrace your inner weirdo? What are you avoiding? Are you failing to launch your business because you're afraid people aren't expecting it from you? Fuck that. Make the decision and then put forth the effort, the energy, and the creativity to see it through until it's a success. Are you going to always be successful? No, but it doesn't matter. Learn from it and gain that invaluable experience so next time a challenge comes along, you'll be wiser. If it doesn't work, at least you gave it a shot and now you know.

Normal people want to put you in a box so they can better understand you. Don't let them. Steve Jobs didn't let anyone put him into a box. Elon Musk hasn't let anyone put him into a box. They're too weird for a box and it's made all the difference in their success. Let it make the difference in your own success as well.

23

PRESSURE IS A PRIVILEGE

I f you haven't learned it by now, you probably need to start reading this book again from the beginning, but the responsibility you have to realize your own success involves more than you. You are also responsible for the success of those in the boat with you. Sometimes that means your friends and coworkers, but it always means your family. You have to be the leader of your family. All this wisdom and the discipline required to make the most of all this wisdom should be a part of the legacy you leave to your children. Everything I'm sharing with you here, I'm also sharing with my kids. Be intentional with the wisdom you share with your kids and if you keep an open mind, you'll discover you can learn a lot by leading. That's why I describe myself as a lead follower of the School of Man. I'm not a guru as much as I am a student of the program.

There's a movement in society today that says we should coddle our children, that we should give them all a participation trophy or a ribbon. I don't buy into that mindset. Some people probably think that makes me an asshole, but I'd argue I'd be more of an asshole if I didn't prepare my kids for success—and failure—in the real world. In my experience, life doesn't always offer participation trophies.

My job as a father is to teach my kids that if you want to get to the top, you've got to bust your ass at practice. A participation trophy might make everyone feel included, but it also devalues the work the kids put in to get to the top. If Ava Madison works really hard on her dance routine and another little girl doesn't even show up to practice, and then they're both given the same ribbon, what lesson did that teach her? In my viewpoint, it's teaching my kid that she can sit around and play video games instead of practicing because everyone's going to end up with the same trophy.

Not in my house. Ashley and I want to prepare my kids for the hard work that life will require of them. I want them to build up their emotional fortitude when the stakes are small—at school yard games and family foot races—so that when the stakes are high—at career checkpoints and professional challenges—they'll be psychologically equipped to deal with success, or failure. Because there will be both. And there will be pressure.

Adults sometimes crack under pressure because they were never taught to handle it as children. It is imperative that we teach our kids that pressure is a privilege.

Why is it a privilege? Because it's an opportunity to live and not exist. It's an opportunity to stretch yourself and as long as you are fighting you are not failing. It's one of the greatest gifts given to us. Don't waste it. Instead, go look for it.

That's what it sounds like in theory; Here's what it looks like in practice:

Landon recently came to me and said he wanted to play baseball. Well, I am not one of those dads that will drag their kid to the ball field. If Landon wants to play, I need him to *want to play*. If I have to drag a kid kicking and screaming to practice, then that kid doesn't actually want to play. In our house, yes, we believe in finishing what we start and honoring our commitments, but if you don't want to go to practice, then it's not worth playing at all. That's why in the beginning, my number one objective from the outset—as soon as he said he wanted to play, before he even got put on a team—was to give it my best shot at getting him to quit. I grabbed our gloves and a bat and some balls and I took him out to the practice field.

"If you don't quit," I told him, "then you've got what it takes to play baseball. And then I'll invest my energy into making you a ball player. I'll love you regardless, even if you quit, but we're going to be at this field two or three times a week to see if it's something you really want to do. We're going to learn the fundamentals before we even step out on the field."

He accepted those terms, and on Day One I dropped the hammer on him. We're talking about a seven-year-old boy, so I'm sure there were people watching and probably noticing that the way I was operating was not something you would find in your parenting books.

Every time he made a bad throw, he had to do 15 burpees. Every time he whined or complained, he had to run. At the end of the day, that's the best way I know how to teach my son. There was plenty of coaching and mentorship at the same time, but I wanted him to know that I expect excellence out of my children. I should be clear here and say excellence does not equal perfection. Every kid makes mistakes. Even professional athletes make mistakes. Mistakes happen, but the only way to get better is to value excellence and punish mistakes in a way that encourages a growth mindset.

As time went on, he got better and better, but more importantly, Landon latched onto the game. He learned to understand that hard work is what generates pretty much everything in our life. It's amazing to me that people with fixed mindsets don't necessarily look at it that way. A growth mindset looks at something and recognizes that it's going to be hard and that it may result in failure, but also that failure is okay because sometimes success doesn't look like the success we generally think of. Sometimes success lies in the learning process. Short-term failure can be part of long-term success.

That's what I was looking for with Landon. Fast-forward to his last game of the fall season. He's playing third base. The batter hits a ground-ball to him and Landon's got the awareness to tag the runner and make the play. Inning over. Then he gets up and we need him to hit.

"Pressure is a privilege," I told him three times if I said it once. "Pressure is a privilege. Pressure is a privilege."

He looked at me and he said, "Dad, I got this."

That was a proud dad moment for me because I knew we'd done all we could to get him ready. If he didn't hit the ball, it wasn't going to be because his nerves were shot. He was emotionally ready. I knew he was going to step into the batter's box and give it hell.

He ended up getting a hit and advancing the runners, and we won the game. The kid is seven years old, but he understood that he was privileged to have the pressure on him when the moment mattered. Granted, Landon hasn't known adversity like most of us adults have, but still, he handled it well and he's on track to do the same when he's an adult.

A lot of us—grown-ups—avoid pressure in all aspects of our lives because at some point in our lives we developed a fear of it. When in actuality we should run toward the pressure because pressure is what generates all the results in our lives. Think about it. The pressure we feel is often the only thing that can motivate us to do the things we know we should—or want—to do. Pressure is a catalyst for positive change. Pressure is a privilege.

I'll never forget when I was in ninth grade in an oral presentation class. In what was probably my first ever oral presentation, I had to speak on how to field a ground ball. That's something I should've been able to do with my eyes closed because at that time I was the starting second basemen on my school's varsity baseball team. But after I gave my presentation, my teacher, Ms. Green, gave me an F.

I immediately started playing the blame game, which is a natural human instinct. We want to preserve our way of thinking and defend ourselves from responsibility. That's why so many of us get into trouble so often. We make mistakes and then we stick by those mistakes out of some kind of misguided sense of loyalty to self. But what you have to remember is that you aren't a failure until you start to blame others. Despite how it initially seemed to me, failing the presentation wasn't the end of the test. It was just the beginning.

Once I accepted the blame for failing the presentation, I understood that I'd have to put forth more effort if I wanted a better grade. That's a lesson I needed to learn, which is why I'm glad Ms. Green failed me. So that I would understand I failed myself. Once I learned that crucial lesson, I worked harder,

I aced the class, and as an adult I now speak in front of rooms full of people all the time. That was a lesson I needed to learn, so I'm glad I learned it early.

Had I instead never accepted responsibility for the grade I earned and instead continued playing the blame game, that would have become my identity for who knows how long. I would've continued through life with a string of failing grades—and the unhappiness that comes with that—convinced someone else had caused it. But the truth is that no one was going to save me from that life, so I had to save myself.

Some people can't handle the pressure of that, but as I said before, pressure is a privilege. Put yourself in situations where the game is on the line. You should want to be the man with the ball in the fourth quarter with ten seconds left on the clock when the game is on the line. Take the shot. And if you miss it... who cares? You're still alive. You're still moving. You're still growing. Have the conversation at work you know you need to have. Everything you want in life comes with pressure, but pressure is not a reason not to have the life you want. Take on the project, apply for the job. You'll never grow if you don't get out of your comfort zone. You'll never make yourself or those around you any better if you don't accept the reality that pressure is a privilege.

So many of us have taken shots in the past and gotten burned and so now we're scared to take more shots. We develop this upper limit effect that makes us believe we don't deserve to be happy because we missed a shot we took once. Once! We all deserve to be happy, but we also deserve to have to work for it. We have to put in the effort to get the things we want.

When Landon said, "Dad, I got this," and stepped into the batter's box, he was demonstrating life without that upper limit

149

effect. Young kids fall down a lot and it's nothing for them to get right back up. They don't think anything of recovering from failure. It's not until our teenage and college years that society indoctrinates us all in the idea that risk is a terrifying thing. That's not true, but that indoctrination process is an effective one because by the time we reach full-grown adulthood, most of us have forgotten that if we fall, we can still get back up.

We don't let our children win in our house until they've earned it so they're ready for the failures they'll eventually face later in life. The human experience is riddled with failures. If a kid has never lost a game in his life, but then gets into higher levels of competition and gets his ass handed to him—how do you think he's going to process that failure? It won't be good.

We're not just talking about children here, which is why this ideology is a key tenet that School of Man preaches as we push the needle. So many guys are dead in their thirties, their forties, their fifties, even though we don't bury them until their eighties. I say it all the time because I see people who need reminding so often. Men who tell themselves they are too old to launch the business they've dreamed about for years or they can never win back their wife's heart. Whatever those dreams are that these guys want to pursue, they are achievable if they want to put in the work. It's just that most people don't.

Audit your life. Figure out where you want to grow, put in the work, embrace the fact that pressure is a privilege, and then live the life you want. There are no shortcuts.

School of Man gives some men a path to the things they want. It helps train them physically, mentally, and emotionally to deal with the pressure they face in the real world. It gives them a sense of accomplishment because the work they put in is hard and it is real. Everyone wants to be a part of School of Man on a sunny day, but when it comes to nut-cutting time and the cadre are putting the screws on you...there are a small percentage of people who have learned to face that pressure with a growth mindset and overcome anything in their path.

Not everyone is meant for School of Man, but men and women alike should find the thing in their lives that will prepare them to face the pressure, to grow, to live the life they want to live. Set yourself up for success.

In this book, I've tried to share with you the experiences and the lessons I've learned in my own life. And also the rebirths I've seen in some of the men who have come through the School of Man. Theirs are just a few of the examples I've seen first-hand of men committing themselves to be better men, better husbands, better fathers, better friends, better sons—the list goes on and on. The roles men play in our lives are countless and the pressure those roles put on them to be who they are supposed to be is immeasurable. But the lion is only scary if it's chasing you. Turn around. Chase the lion. And have a plan for when you catch it.

9 781953 153494